Log and Timber Frame Homes

Log and Timber Frame Homes

Tina Skinner

Schiffer
Publishing Ltd

4880 Lower Valley Road, Atglen, PA 19310 USA

LIBRARY OF CONGRESS CATALOGING-IN-PUBLICATION DATA

SKINNER, TINA.
LOG AND TIMBER FRAME HOMES / BY TINA SKINNER.
P. CM.
ISBN: 0-7643-1754-7
1. WOODEN-FRAME BUILDINGS--DESIGNS AND PLANS. 2. LOG CABINS--DESIGNS
AND PLANS. 3. ARCHITECTURE, DOMESTIC--DESIGNS AND PLANS. I. TITLE.
NA4110 .S55 2002
728.7'3--DC21
2002153159

ALL FLOOR PLANS © HEARTHSTONE, INC.

DESIGNED BY BONNIE M. HENSLEY
COVER DESIGN BY BRUCE M. WATERS
TYPE SET IN P22 CEZANNE REGULAR/ZURICH LTCN BT

ISBN: 0-7643-1754-7
PRINTED IN CHINA

PUBLISHED BY SCHIFFER PUBLISHING LTD.
4880 LOWER VALLEY ROAD
ATGLEN, PA 19310
PHONE: (610) 593-1777; FAX: (610) 593-2002
E-MAIL: SCHIFFERBK@AOL.COM
PLEASE VISIT OUR WEB SITE CATALOG AT WWW.SCHIFFERBOOKS.COM
WE ARE ALWAYS LOOKING FOR PEOPLE TO WRITE BOOKS ON NEW AND RELATED
SUBJECTS. IF YOU HAVE AN IDEA FOR A BOOK PLEASE CONTACT US AT THE ABOVE
ADDRESS.

THIS BOOK MAY BE PURCHASED FROM THE PUBLISHER.
INCLUDE $3.95 FOR SHIPPING.
PLEASE TRY YOUR BOOKSTORE FIRST.
YOU MAY WRITE FOR A FREE CATALOG.

IN EUROPE, SCHIFFER BOOKS ARE DISTRIBUTED BY
BUSHWOOD BOOKS
6 MARKSBURY AVE.
KEW GARDENS
SURREY TW9 4JF ENGLAND
PHONE: 44 (0) 20 8392-8585; FAX: 44 (0) 20 8392-9876
E-MAIL: BUSHWD@AOL.COM
FREE POSTAGE IN THE U.K., EUROPE; AIR MAIL AT COST.

Dedication

To Stephen and Niki —
MAY YOU FIND YOUR HAPPINESS ON THIS DIFFICULT JOURNEY.

Foreword

While I was in graduate school in the late 1970s, I read a fascinating article about the re-birth of heavy timber construction. Intrigued, I kept up with that trade as well as the growing market for log homes. Not long after that, I actually sought out the best log home company I could – for my own home.

During that process, I found a wonderful small company called Hearthstone. They featured a style that was a reproduction of the way the best log homes were actually built in the 1700s and 1800s, and their reputation was impeccable. I was hooked on the homes and became hooked on the business.

After getting to know the owner, we eventually came to an arrangement that would both employ me – and give me the opportunity to own Hearthstone. I never really knew just how big an opportunity and blessing that agreement would become. In many ways, more than twenty years later, I still don't know yet how big a blessing it was, because it grows and I learn more every day.

Hearthstone – and the overall world of log and heavy timber construction – is not just a business. It truly is a way of life, an environment, and in some ways a non-stop vacation. We have to be serious about running our business, but it is also a creative piece of "art-in-progress". We invent, create, and carry out products, homes, and commercial structures of the most extraordinary sort. And as we travel that path, we help nurture and develop the passions, skills, and dreams of employees, architects, engineers, builders, and – of course – our clients.

At Hearthstone – above all else – we are unshakably committed to the nearly lost art and trade of the Timberwright. Because of this defining promise, we can proudly serve our clients in that most fulfilling of human aspirations: the quest for a truly extraordinary home and living environment.

Randy Giles
Owner, Hearthstone, Inc.

Contents

Introduction

Vast stretches of virgin forest were the true pot of gold awaiting settlers to North America. Timberwrights from Europe brought their centuries-old craft to the New World, and hand-hewed great timbers for log home and great timber framed bridges, barns, churches, and public buildings — architectural legacies that live on.

Hearthstone is a company that got its start restoring these wooden wonders. Running out of original material to satisfy their customer's demand, they relearned a lost art and began building from scratch. What you see here is the marriage of modern technology with an ancient craft. Hearthstone timberwrights relearned this art, and now employ themselves housing customers who seek the very best.

The old-world art of the timberwright – the ability to precisely cut, hew, and erect an incredibly durable and strong structure with mortise and tenon joinery and wood pegs – was replaced late in the 19th century by structural steel, dimensional lumber, and wire nails. With it went the wonder of whole trees turned into a thing of beauty, a form of folk architecture that appeals to today's homeowners.

Today's homeowner is looking for something distinct and exciting; a home of imagination, character, and traditional excellence. Many find this by looking back, rather than forward, when choosing a basic framework for their domestic lives.

Timber frame homes make a majestic statement. The beautiful, structural elements of the home are left exposed on the interior for breathtaking effect. The exteriors are wrapped in a blanket of foam core panels and siding of the owner's choice, making the building as comfortable and energy efficient as any other.

Log homes provide their own amazing insulation against the outside elements and noise, with thickness of up to 8 inches and lengths up to 40 feet. Further, there's no wall more wondrous than one of raw forest, of majestic giant logs that bespeak years of solid growth and beauty. The logs shown in this book are hand-hewn, the edges chamfered for soft effect, and stacked for a unique beauty that draws admiration for the craftsman.

This book takes a look at the bold, inspiring statements wood makes in domestic architecture. Log homes, timber frame homes, and homes that combine both arts are explored inside and out. Floor plans provide insight into the workings of the home, with the result that one might begin to imagine themselves living in such a place. The next step in the journey, of course, is planning such a place, buying a plot of land, and then building. Once you've poured over these pages, you may be inevitably upon your way.

Forested Away

This couple built their home to last for a hundred years when they planned their rural retirement. The house looks as though it already predates its occupants by a hundred years, but don't be fooled by the solid construction. Inside their brand new home, the happy owners have assembled furnishings perfect for a mountain cabin, yet elegant enough in their simplicity for a lifetime of accumulated tastes.

Green gingerbread trim adds a touch of Victorian flair to this log home. Everything about this home — from the river stone chimney and foundation to the massive logs — screams historic treasure. It will be someday!

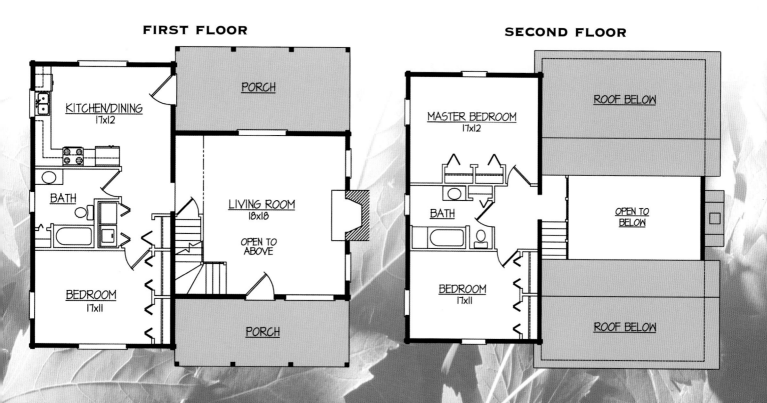

FIRST FLOOR

PORCH

KITCHEN/DINING
17x12

BATH

LIVING ROOM
18x18

OPEN TO
ABOVE

BEDROOM
17x11

PORCH

SECOND FLOOR

ROOF BELOW

MASTER BEDROOM
17x12

BATH

OPEN TO
BELOW

BEDROOM
17x11

ROOF BELOW

11—

A BEAR SKIN AND OTHER PELTS WERE SCATTERED THROUGHOUT THE HOME, ALONG WITH BEAR ART AND PRIMITIVE ANTIQUES AND FURNISHINGS. ALL COMPLEMENT THE STONE AND WOOD, LOVINGLY DISPLAYED THROUGH THE HOME, AND NOWHERE MORE IMPRESSIVE THAN IN THE OPEN LIVING AREA, WHERE A CATHEDRAL CEILING FLOATS ATOP MASSIVE TIMBERS AND A STONE CHIMNEY.

STONE FLOORS IN BOTH OF THE HOME'S FULL BATHS
ARE IN KEEPING WITH SOLID WOOD CONSTRUCTION.
THE BEDROOMS ARE LOVINGLY, AND PATRIOTICALLY,
APPOINTED.

13

Garden Centerpiece

Set like a gem amidst a lovingly tended landscape, this log structure culminates its owners' passion for home. Made of wood and stone, it sets like an Early American sculpture amidst flowering beds. Visitors often ask if the house is a historic property. It isn't, but it is sure to be a family heirloom.

F&E Schmidt Photography

FIRST FLOOR

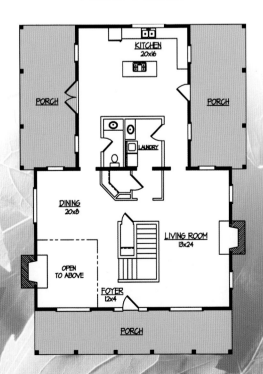

KITCHEN
20x16

PORCH

PORCH

LAUNDRY

DINING
20x8

LIVING ROOM
13x24

OPEN
TO ABOVE

FOYER
12x4

PORCH

SECOND FLOOR

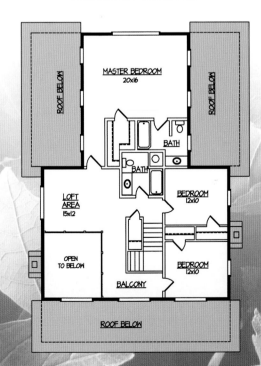

ROOF BELOW

MASTER BEDROOM
20x16

ROOF BELOW

BATH

BATH

LOFT
AREA
15x12

BEDROOM
12x10

OPEN
TO BELOW

BEDROOM
12x10

BALCONY

ROOF BELOW

WOODEN SHINGLES, ENORMOUS LOGS, AND AUTHENTIC DESIGN CREATE THE ILLUSION OF AN HISTORIC LANDMARK. THE FLOWER BEDS AND IMMACULATE LAWN ARE TESTAMENT TO THE OWNER'S UNDYING LOVE OF LIVING HERE. A GARAGE HAS BEEN SEALED OFF, THE DRIVE-WAY REROUTED TO KEEP AUTO-MOBILES OUT OF THIS PLEASANT, TIMELESS PICTURE.

F&E Schmidt Photography

F&E Schmidt Photography

FROM GROUND LEVEL, YOU WOULDN'T NOTICE THESE LARGE WINDOWS AND FRENCH DOORS TUCKED UNDER THE OVERHANGING EAVES. HOWEVER, THEIR PRESENCE MAKES THE INTERIOR SO MUCH LIGHTER THAN THE TINY TRADITIONAL WINDOWS ALLOWED BY LOG HOME CONSTRUCTION.

AN OVERHANGING ROOF ALLOWS FOR BOTH OPEN AND SCREENED-IN PORCH
AREAS; FREQUENT HAUNTS FOR THESE GARDEN LOVERS.

Rising Above It All

Set on sturdy stilts, this log home elevates its owners above ocean tides on the Gulf coast, and affords them a view across the dunes. To give their home more of a seaside feel, the logs were finished inside with a clear stain that softens the effect and works well with the pastels and summer colors suitable to seaside vacations. As one might expect, much of the family's focus is on the porches fore and aft, where they can smell the salty air and listen to the surf. Weather not permitting, though, there's a large living room set off like a winter retreat, complete with a cozy wood burning stove for warmth.

Ken Krakow Photography

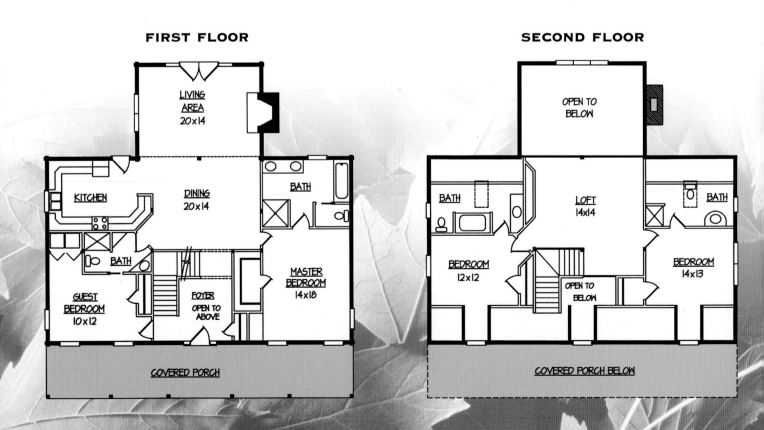

FIRST FLOOR

LIVING AREA 20x14

KITCHEN

DINING 20x14

BATH

BATH

MASTER BEDROOM 14x18

GUEST BEDROOM 10x12

FOYER OPEN TO ABOVE

COVERED PORCH

SECOND FLOOR

OPEN TO BELOW

BATH

LOFT 14x14

BATH

BEDROOM 12x12

OPEN TO BELOW

BEDROOM 14x13

COVERED PORCH BELOW

IN THE ABSENCE OF TIDAL WAVES, THE RAISED AREA BELOW THIS BEACH HOUSE IS IDEAL FOR PARKING.
ELEVATING THE LIVING QUARTERS ALSO IMPROVED THE VIEWS FOR THESE PART-TIME ISLAND DWELLERS.

A LOFT OVERLOOKS THE LIVING AREA, WHICH IN TURN FACES A COVERED PORCH. ENORMOUS BEAMS SUPPORT THE WEIGHT ABOVE, AND ALLOW FOR A CATHEDRAL CEILING.

A LOFT HAS BEEN CLAIMED BY THE LADY OF THE HOUSE FOR USE AS A PRIVATE RETREAT. ALL IT WANTS IS A JUICY NOVEL TO MAKE IT COMPLETE.

THE MASTER BEDROOM IS SPACIOUS, COMPLETE WITH A
PRIVATE BATH. THREE OTHER ROOMS WERE ADDED FOR
FREQUENT VISITS BY FAMILY AND GUESTS.

21

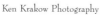

Mixing Business and Pleasure

ENORMOUS LOGS HEWN FROM EASTERN WHITE PINE DEFINE
THE LENGTH OF THIS TWO-STORY HOME.

FIRST FLOOR

SECOND FLOOR

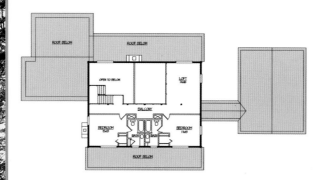

Years of planning went into this semi-retirement home, culminating in a dream retreat where the couple continues to work out of a home office, to be productive in a garage workshop, and to kick back in rocking chairs front and back. A first-floor master suite and covered breezeway between garage and the main floor simplify life. A second floor was added to provide an inviting loft and guest accommodations, but trips up aren't mandatory as the couple ages.

A WATERFALL OFF THE FRONT PORCH PROVIDES HOURS OF BACKGROUND MUSIC FOR PORCH DWELLERS

A FIREPLACE WARMS A HOME OFFICE AND LIBRARY, WHERE WORK CALLS WHEN THE WEATHER IS INCLEMENT.

Roger Wade Photography

KITCHEN AND DINING
AREAS ARE CONTAINED
IN ONE LONG STRETCH
OF ROOM, WHERE THE
HOMEOWNERS CAN
SETTLE IN FOR
INFORMAL DINING AT
THE ISLAND COUNTER,
OR ENTERTAIN IN
STYLE BY A PICTURE
WINDOW.

25—

Roger Wade Photography

AN EXPANSIVE GREAT ROOM WITH A HEAVY TIMBER CATHEDRAL ROOF SYSTEM FOCUSES ON A STONE HEARTH. A LOFT OVERLOOKS THE SCENE.

Roger Wade Photography

AN ADDITIONAL UPSTAIRS BEDROOM, ACROSS FROM THE MASTER SUITE, BECKONS GROWN CHILDREN OR AND GRANDCHILDREN TO VISIT WHILE PROVIDING STORAGE SPACE.

Roger Wade Photography

Originally built as a weekend home, these homeowners realized their dream and moved in full-time. They didn't leave the world, or all their income, behind — the loft was converted to a home office. However, trips away became infrequent, the "full-time home" was closed, and all the couple's favorite furnishings and antiques were brought along to what is now their full-time heaven in the mountains. They left plenty of room for the kids to come back on weekends, too, with two spare bedrooms.

FIRST FLOOR   **SECOND FLOOR**

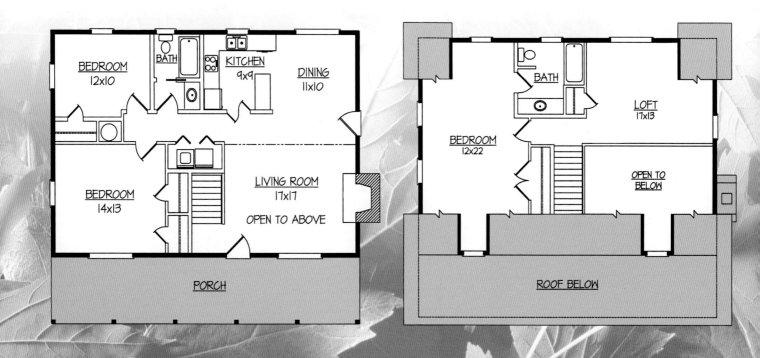

F&E Schmidt Photography

ROCKERS WELCOME
EMPTY NESTERS HOME
NIGHTLY TO THEIR
FORMER MOUNTAIN
RETREAT. A SCREENED-
IN PORCH WAS ADDED
OFF THE DINING ROOM,
OPENING A VIEW OF THE
PEACEFUL FOREST
BEYOND.

F&E Schmidt Photography

F&E Schmidt Photography

THESE HOMEOWNERS KNOW WHAT THEY'RE ALL ABOUT, AND THEIR DÉCOR REFLECTS IT. THEIR HOME IS FURNISHED IN OUTDOORS ANTIQUES AND MEMORABILIA, AND INFUSED WITH RURAL SENTIMENT.

F&E Schmidt Photography

F&E Schmidt Photography

31 ——

SPORTS ANTIQUES DECORATE THIS RUSTIC LOG CABIN. A HEAVY
TIMBER CATHEDRAL CEILING ALLOWS THE LIVING ROOM TO SOAR
TWO STORIES HIGH, OVERLOOKED BY A SECOND-FLOOR LOFT.

F&E Schmidt Photography

A FORMAL DINING ROOM WOULD SEEM AS OUT OF CONTEXT IN THIS MOUNTAIN HOME AS A WOOD-PANELED STUDY. INSTEAD, THE KITCHEN AND DINING ROOM COMMUNICATE OPENLY, AND FOOD PREPARATION OFTEN MOVES TO THE TABLE WHEN MORE COUNTER SPACE IS NEEDED.

A DRAFTING TABLE AND DESK ALLOW THE HOME OWNER TO WORK FROM HOME, SEMI-RETIRED AND FAR FROM THE BUSTLE OF A FORMER LIFE.

Quilts and other textiles reflect a feminine touch.

Weekend Ranch

A FAMILY GETAWAY, THIS ONE WORKS OFF A CENTRAL
LIVING AREA FLANKED BY SLEEPING QUARTERS.

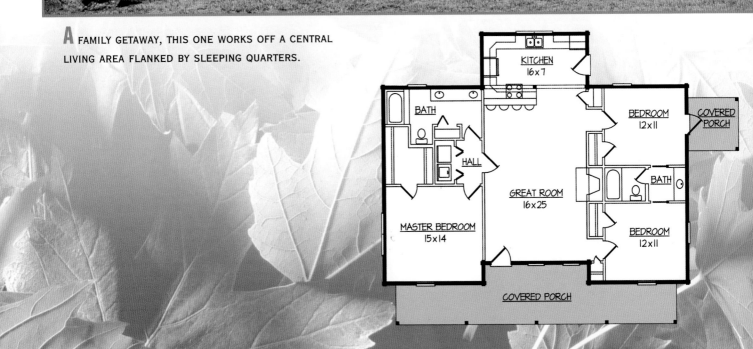

KITCHEN
16 x 7

BATH

BEDROOM
12 x 11

COVERED
PORCH

HALL

GREAT ROOM
16 x 25

BATH

MASTER BEDROOM
15 x 14

BEDROOM
12 x 11

COVERED PORCH

This one-story home was designed for a busy family looking for intimate family getaways that include aging parents, grandchildren, and pets. The vaulted, central living area is flanked by bedrooms on both sides. The living, dining, and kitchen areas were blended to create an open, flowing environment, allowing for greater interaction between family members. Masters of the home, the owners enjoy their own private wing, accessed by a short hall that gives them privacy and opens to a private bath.

Ken Krakow Photography

A COVERED PORCH IS A HANDY OUTDOOR RETREAT, ESPECIALLY WHEN THE RAUCOUS OF VISITING FAMILY MEMBERS OVERWHELMS THE GENEROUS INDOOR SPACE.

Ken Krakow Photography

36

A CENTRAL LIVING AREA FOCUSES ON THE FIREPLACE. A LOFT IS A POPULAR CHILDREN'S FORT ON ONE SIDE, TOPPING THE ENTRYWAY TO TWO GUEST ROOMS. THE KITCHEN OPENS OUT TO THE LIVING AND DINING SPACES, KEEPING THE COOK IN COMMUNICATION WITH THE ACTION.

THE MASTER BEDROOM IN-CLUDES A LITTLE EXTRA INDOOR RETREAT ROOM, THOUGH THE HOUSE WAS DESIGNED FOR TOGETHERNESS. YOUNGER VISITORS BUNK UP IN A ROOM BUILT FOR FUN AND WHIS-PERING LONG AFTER THE LAST "SHUSH." THE POINT OF A FAMILY VACATION HOME, AFTER ALL, IS FOR THE FAMILY TO BE TOGETHER.

Light Living

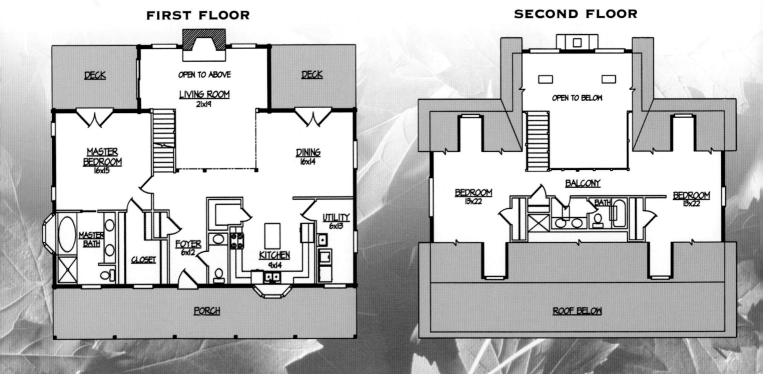

FIRST FLOOR

DECK

OPEN TO ABOVE

DECK

LIVING ROOM
21x19

MASTER
BEDROOM
16x15

DINING
16x14

UTILITY
6x13

MASTER
BATH

CLOSET

FOYER
6x12

KITCHEN
4x14

PORCH

SECOND FLOOR

OPEN TO BELOW

BEDROOM
13x22

BALCONY

BATH

BEDROOM
13x22

ROOF BELOW

These homeowners chose a log home design that allows them to incorporate enormous picture windows in rooms where lots of light and view were wanted. Their focus was always toward the outdoors – with private decks, a sunroom, and a full-length front porch allowing themselves as much space as possible to play outdoors, or in close proximity. The result is a true stand-out addition to a large-tract subdivision.

SET ON A STONE FOUNDATION, THE LOWER LEVEL IS DEDICATED TO THE GARAGE AND WORKSHOP AREAS. UPSTAIRS, THE ROOMS FOCUS OUT ON PORCH AND PRIVATE DECKS.

A FULL-LENGTH VERANDA PROVIDES ENTRY TO THIS SPACIOUS HOME. INDOORS, A BENCH WAITS TO HELP YOU EASE OFF YOUR SHOES.

F&E Schmidt Photography

WEATHER PERMITTING, DINING MOVES
OUTDOORS TO A COMFY SCREENED-IN PORCH.

F&E Schmidt Photography

Dark wood finish on kitchen cabinetry adds drama to a wood-beamed kitchen. White countertop and finished walls create contrast.

45

THE MASTER BEDROOM, LIKE THE REST OF THE HOME, IS FOCUSED OUTDOORS. A PRIVATE DECK IS A PERFECT PLACE FOR MORNING COFFEE, OR A GOODNIGHT WISH ON A STAR. EVEN THE MASTER BATHROOM ENJOYS A TON OF NATURAL LIGHTING. A BAY WINDOW BY THE BATHTUB INVITES ONE TO LINGER BY THE VIEW.

HEAVY BEAMS CROSS THE CATHEDRAL CEILING IN THIS INVITING LIVING ROOM.

TWIN BEDS FLANK AN AMAZING DOME-TOP WINDOW THAT DOMINATES ONE OF TWO LOFTY BEDROOMS.

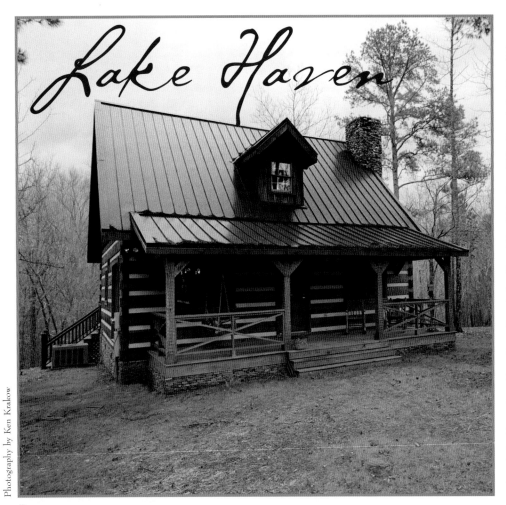

Photography by Ken Krakow

Lake Haven

Built on a heavenly plot of land, a cool mountain stream running across the property, this home is remote from the world and close to a scenic mountain lake. An ideal getaway. The owners designed a home that harmonizes with its surroundings. With its simple log exterior and red tin roof, it might have been built here a hundred years ago. Yet it's stocked and furnished for modern comfort, and inside it's a real showplace. The two-story living room features a fieldstone chimney quarried locally, and the artwork sets the stage for the wild surrounds.

A SIMPLE CABIN IN APPEARANCE, THIS SECOND HOME CAN SLEEP SIX COMFORTABLY AND INCLUDES A TWO-STORY LIVING ROOM. WINDOWS WERE SMALL TO MAINTAIN A TRADITIONAL LOG HOME LOOK.

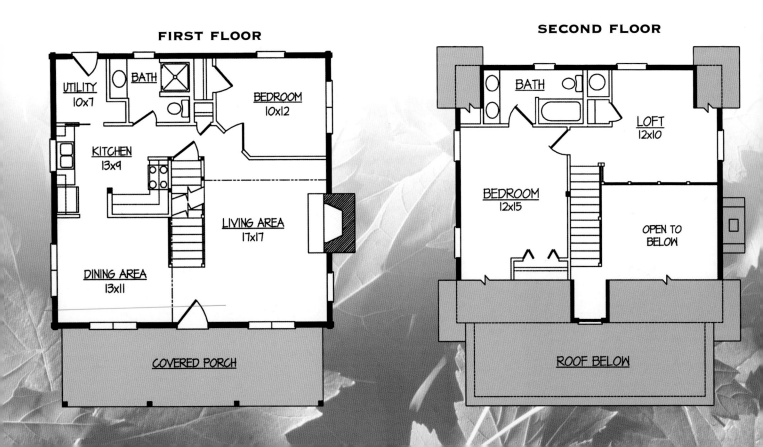

FIRST FLOOR

UTILITY
10x7

BATH

BEDROOM
10x12

KITCHEN
13x9

LIVING AREA
17x17

DINING AREA
13x11

COVERED PORCH

SECOND FLOOR

BATH

LOFT
12x10

BEDROOM
12x15

OPEN TO BELOW

ROOF BELOW

Photography by Ken Krakow

ALL EYES ARE ON THE GORGEOUS FIREPLACE, EVEN THE FURRY ONES IN THE FORM OF HUNTING TROPHIES. LEATHER FURNISHINGS ARE A NATURAL GO-WITH FOR WOOD AND STONE ARCHITECTURE.

49

Photography by Ken Krakow

KITCHEN AND DINING ROOM COMMUNICATE DIRECTLY ACROSS A HALF-WALL OF CABINETS AND COUNTERS. WHITE APPLIANCES AND LIGHTING PROVIDE CLEAN CONTRAST TO PINE CABINETRY AND WOODEN WALLS AND FLOOR.

Photography by Ken Krakow

Extra bunks are available in the loft, with a private powder room. The master bedroom dominates the second floor.

Wooded Ridge

F&E Schmidt

FIRST FLOOR

GARAGE
23x23

WORKSHOP
13x10

UTILITY

DINING
12x11

KITCHEN
10x16

LAUNDRY

STORAGE
UNDER
STAIRS

PORCH

MASTER BATH

WALK-IN
CLOSET

GREAT ROOM
16x43

OPEN TO ABOVE

MASTER BEDROOM
17x20

OPEN TO ABOVE

PORCH

SECOND FLOOR

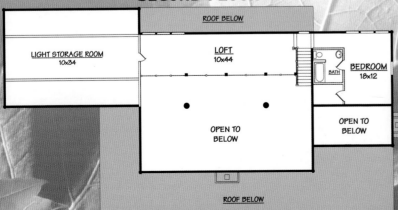

ROOF BELOW

LIGHT STORAGE ROOM
10x34

LOFT
10x44

BATH

BEDROOM
18x12

OPEN TO
BELOW

OPEN TO
BELOW

ROOF BELOW

The homeowners wanted a getaway that blended in with the natural surroundings. Perched on a gentle hill, this hunting retreat quietly emerges from a forest of fir trees. The soft slope of the front roof conceals a massive great room comprising the hub of the rustic, timber cabin. Covered porches flank the front and rear of the home, greatly expanding living areas to the forest and country beyond.

53—

F&E Schmidt

A PROMINENT FRONT PORCH ALLOWS FOR EXPANSIVE VIEWS OF THE
SURROUNDING HILLSIDE. GRACEFULLY ANGLED SKYWARD, THE ROOF
MAINTAINS THE EQUANIMITY OF THE RIDGE LINE.

LOCAL ARTIFACTS, INCLUD-
ING A NATIVE AMERICAN
TOTEM POLE, HEIGHTEN THE
DRAMA OF A PAIR OF
BEAUTIFULLY DISTRESSED,
MASSIVE WOODEN DOORS AT
THE MAIN ENTRANCE TO THE
CABIN.

WITH ITS SOARING
HEAVY TIMBER
CATHEDRAL CEILING
AND GENEROUS
LENGTH, THE GREAT
ROOM DOMINATES
THE FLOOR PLAN OF
THE CABIN. RICH
WOOD TONES
THROUGHOUT
PROVIDE RUSTIC
CHARM.

OPENING TO THE EXPANSE
OF THE GREAT ROOM, THE
KITCHEN AND ITS ADJACENT
DINING AREA FEEL COZIER
WITH LOWER CEILINGS
PROVIDED BY THE LOFT
ABOVE.

F&E Schmidt

THE GENTLE ANGLE OF THE FRONT-FACING ROOF GIVES THE UPSTAIRS LOFT MORE SPACE AND PRIVACY
THAN MOST. SKYLIGHTS BATHE THE ROUGH-HEWN STRUCTURAL TIMBER IN WARM LIGHT.

A SPACIOUS MASTER BEDROOM AND
BATH EXTEND OFF THE GREAT ROOM.

F&E Schmidt

Barn Again

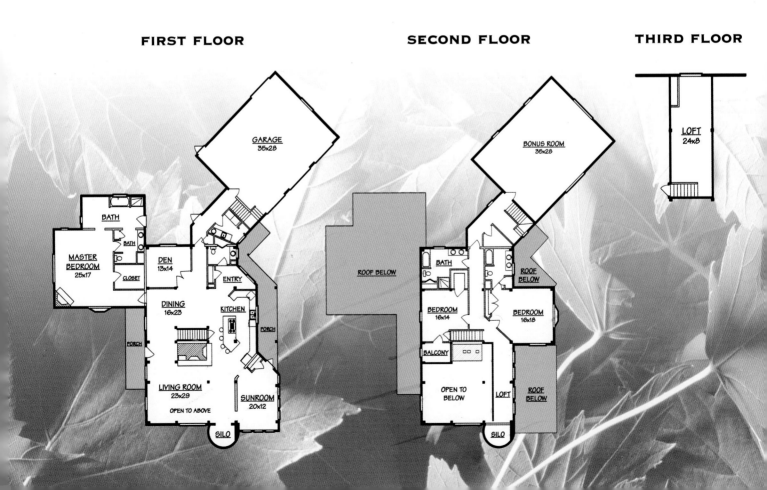

FIRST FLOOR

SECOND FLOOR

THIRD FLOOR

GARAGE
35x28

BONUS ROOM
35x28

LOFT
24x8

BATH

BATH

MASTER
BEDROOM
25x17

DEN
13x14

CLOSET

ENTRY

ROOF BELOW

BATH

ROOF
BELOW

DINING
16x23

KITCHEN

PORCH

BEDROOM
16x14

BEDROOM
16x18

PORCH

BALCONY

LIVING ROOM
23x29

SUNROOM
20x12

OPEN TO ABOVE

OPEN TO
BELOW

LOFT

ROOF
BELOW

SILO

SILO

Drawing inspiration from the historic farms near this rural Pennsylvania site, the homeowners felt a barn would fit beautifully into the landscape. Together they came up with a timber frame structure, with a log master bedroom suite. A grain silo was incorporated into the design and, to complete the barn feel, a cupola vent was installed atop the adjoining red metal roof, complete with a vintage weather vane. The many multiform windows of the front façade, however, clearly connote a sense of home while also flooding the ample interior with lots of light.

GRAY STAIN FINISH ON THE EXPOSED BOARDS AND BEAMS UNITES WITH THE SLATE FLOOR AND MUTED FURNISHINGS TO CREATE AN INTIMATE SUNROOM ADJACENT TO THE FRONT ENTRANCE. THE SERENITY OF THIS DESIGN COMPLEMENTS VIEWS OF THE LOCAL FARM COMMUNITY.

DRAMA IS PROVIDED BY SOARING CEILINGS,
WINDOWS AND EXPOSED HEARTHSTONES AND
BEAMS IN THE MAIN LIVING AREA.

61

CLASSIC COUNTRY AND
AMERICANA DÉCOR ARE
APTLY APPLIED
THROUGHOUT THE
KITCHEN AND ADJOINING
DINING AREA. BOR-
ROWED FROM THE
LOCAL ARTICHOKE
HARVEST, THE VIBRANT
GREEN COLOR OF THE
WAINSCOTING GIVES THE
ROOM TRUE FARM
SPIRIT.

DISTRESSED TIMBER BEAMS AND CHINKING PROVIDE THE MASTER SUITE WITH THE AMBIENCE OF A RUSTIC LOG CABIN. OUTSIDE THE BEDROOM, A BALCONY IS THE PERFECT PLACE TO STUDY THE LINES OF EXPOSED TIMBER FRAMING.

SUBTLE CURVES IN THE FINISH DETAIL SOFTEN AND
HARMONIZE THE NATURAL ELEMENTS OF THE HOME.

F&E Schmidt Photography

FIRST FLOOR

SECOND FLOOR

DECK

KEEPING ROOM
10x21

SCREENED
PORCH

KITCHEN
14x16

FAMILY ROOM
15x21

BATH

GARAGE
24x24

BREEZEWAY

MASTER BEDROOM
14x17

LAUNDRY

GREAT ROOM
20x21

PORCH

OPEN TO ABOVE

PORCH

ROOF BELOW

BEDROOM
28x16

LOFT
15x21

BATH

BEDROOM
19x15

OPEN TO BELOW

This adaptation of a classic woodcutters cottage provides roomy haven for a family who wanted to nestle their home amidst a Missouri forest clearing. White, wide bead chinking stands out like icing against the darker, hand hewn timbers. The predominant fieldstone chimney conveys a warmth overall while candles in the windows gently invite us to step inside the charming house.

THE MAIN LIVING AREA WITH KITCHEN BEYOND OPENS TO A GREAT ROOM. TO ACHIEVE THE WOODSY LOOK THEY CRAVED, THE HOMEOWNERS OPTED FOR A NATURAL, OILED FINISH TO THE TIMBERS INSIDE.

F&E Schmidt Photography

WINDOWS PROFILE THE CHIMNEY AND FRAME
A COLLECTION OF ANTIQUE FARMING IMPLE-
MENTS WITH VIEWS OF TREES.

WITH THE VIEW OF SUMMER FOLIAGE IN THE
BATHROOM, ONE GETS THE DISTINCT NOTION OF
WASHING UP IN THE TREETOPS.

F&E Schmidt Photography

TIMBER TRUSSES ALLOW THE USE OF AN
EXPOSED ROOF SYSTEM THAT PROVIDES A
BEAUTIFUL FOCAL POINT IN THE BEDROOMS
UPSTAIRS.

Hilltop Hybrid

Harley Ferguson Photography

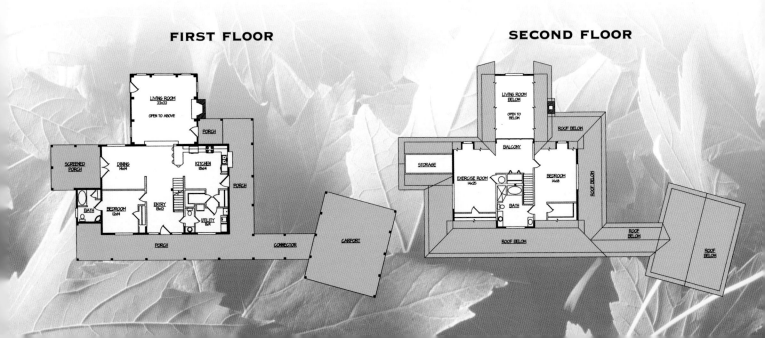

FIRST FLOOR

LIVING ROOM
22x22

OPEN TO ABOVE

PORCH

SCREENED
PORCH

DINING
14x14

KITCHEN
18x14

PORCH

BATH

BEDROOM
12x14

ENTRY
13x12

UTILITY
8x6

PORCH

CONNECTOR

CARPORT

SECOND FLOOR

LIVING ROOM
BELOW

OPEN TO
BELOW

ROOF BELOW

STORAGE

BALCONY

ROOF BELOW

EXERCISE ROOM
14x25

BEDROOM
14x18

BATH

ROOF BELOW

ROOF BELOW

ROOF
BELOW

ROOF
BELOW

This split-personality house roosts on a hill in rural North Carolina. In front, the structure resembles the traditional cabins of the surrounding hill country. Behind, a dramatically angled addition makes a modernist statement overlooking the beautiful rolling foothills of the Blue Ridge Mountains. Combining log and timber frame construction allows the architectural transition and also compliments the natural terrain of the hillside.

WRAPPED AROUND THE FRONT OF THE HOUSE, A BIG COVERED PORCH GIVES GUESTS A GREAT FIRST IMPRESSION. WOODEN ROCKING CHAIRS CREATE A WARM AND INVITING FEEL WHILE THE TRIANGULAR WINDOWS FRAMING THE FRONT DOOR PROVIDE A SPECTACULAR ENTRANCE.

FROM THE FOYER, ACCESS TO OTHER AREAS OF THE HOME RADIATE OUT IN ALL
DIRECTIONS. AN OPEN STAIRWAY LEADS TO THE UPPER FLOOR BALCONY THAT
FACES THE LIVING ROOM.

Harley Ferguson Photography Harley Ferguson Photography

A COUNTRY KITCHEN OPPOSITE THE DINING AREA INCLUDES AN ISLAND AND A BREAKFAST BAR TO OPEN THE SPACE ON BOTH SIDES. GUESTS IN THE GREAT ROOM CAN EASILY PULL UP A STOOL AND KEEP THE HOMEOWNERS HAPPY AS THEY COOK.

Harley Ferguson Photography

THE PERFECT BACK-DROP TO A HUTCH FILLED WITH FINE-CHINA, ONE STARK WHITE WALL ADDS A TOUCH OF FORMALITY TO THE LOG-CABIN FEEL IN THE DINING ROOM.

THE GREAT ROOM FEATURES A WALL OF WINDOWS TO CAPTURE THE PANORAMIC VIEW.

Harley Ferguson Photography

THE UPPER LEVEL HOUSES THE MASTER SUITE AS WELL AS A SPACIOUS HOME OFFICE/EXERCISE ROOM. EASTERN WHITE PINE COMPRISES THE CEILING; THE HOMEOWNERS OPTED FOR A NATURAL FINISH TO MAXIMIZE THE SENSE OF HEIGHT BENEATH THE LOW-SLUNG EAVES.

73

Equestrian Style

F&E Schmidt Photography

BARN: FIRST FLOOR

BARN: SECOND FLOOR

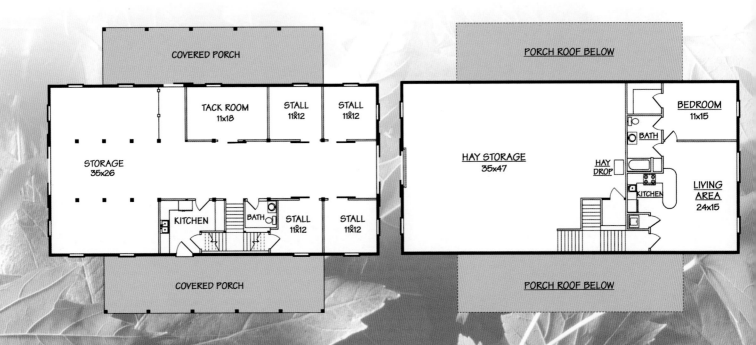

BARN: FIRST FLOOR

COVERED PORCH

STORAGE
35x26

TACK ROOM
11x18

STALL
11x12

STALL
11x12

KITCHEN

BATH

STALL
11x12

STALL
11x12

COVERED PORCH

BARN: SECOND FLOOR

PORCH ROOF BELOW

HAY STORAGE
35x47

HAY
DROP

KITCHEN

BATH

BEDROOM
11x15

LIVING
AREA
24x15

PORCH ROOF BELOW

F&E Schmidt Photography

Comprised of three, unique log structures, this farm complex accommodates a family of avid pheasant hunters and equestrians. The main cabin had to harmonize with the gentle curves of the surrounding Alabama hillside. It sits low and stately on the rise. Dormers in the front and back bring light into the living room and its cozy upstairs loft while breaking up the exterior line of the house. The smaller addition to the side houses a large banquet room where family and friends can enjoy spoils of the hunt. Nearby, a spacious barn keeps the four-legged visitors happy.

F&E Schmidt Photography

THE LIVING ROOM WITH ITS TALL CEILINGS AND RUSTIC CONSTRUCTION PROVIDES THE PERFECT BACKDROP TO THE FAMILY'S HUNTING MEMORABILIA.

A TWO-STORY BARN CREATES A LIGHT AND OPEN ENVIRONMENT FOR EQUESTRIAN ACTIVITIES. INSIDE, A WAGON-WHEEL CHANDELIER PROVIDES CENTRAL LIGHTING ALONG WITH SCONCES.

F&E Schmidt Photography

ONE OF MANY GUEST ROOMS OPENS TO AN ENCLOSED PORCH.

F&E Schmidt Photography

A BANQUET ROOM PLAYS HOST TO HUNTING PARTY FEASTS.

Back in Time

F&E Schmidt Photography

FIRST FLOOR

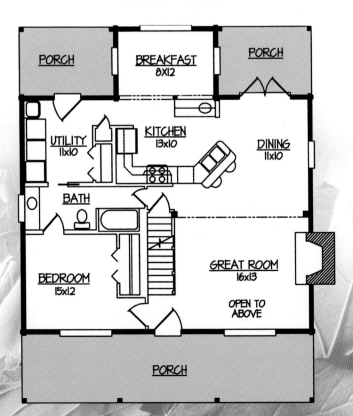

PORCH

BREAKFAST
8X12

PORCH

UTILITY
11x10

KITCHEN
13x10

DINING
11x10

BATH

BEDROOM
15x12

GREAT ROOM
16x13

OPEN TO
ABOVE

PORCH

SECOND FLOOR

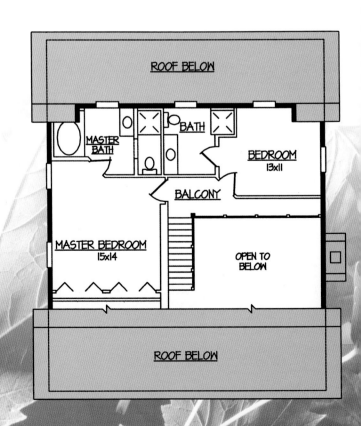

ROOF BELOW

MASTER
BATH

BATH

BEDROOM
13x11

BALCONY

MASTER BEDROOM
15x14

OPEN TO
BELOW

ROOF BELOW

F&E Schmidt Photography

You might feel as though you've stepped back in time, to a Walden's pond home. Here massive logs make up what looks like a simple structure, capped by a green tin roof. Appearances can be deceiving, though. Inside a great room soars two stories high, and thre ample bedrooms attest to the roomy spaces to be found in this happy home. Covered porches offer views of the driveway as well as the lake behind.

F&E Schmidt Photography

LIKE A CABIN FIT FOR EDEN, THIS RUSTIC, LAKESIDE HIDEAWAY ACTUALLY HOUSES A FAMILY OF FOUR WITH EASE.

MASSIVE TIMBERS WERE DOVETAIL JOINTED FOR AN IMPRESSIVE DISPLAY THROUGHOUT THE HOME.

SIMPLE WOOD PLANK CABINETRY ADDS TO THE RUSTIC CHARM OF THE KITCHEN.

83—

THIS LITTLE BREAKFAST NOOK IS ONE OF THE MORE POPULAR SPOTS IN THE HOME. AN ENORMOUS PICTURE
WINDOW OPENS A LAKEFRONT VISTA, AND THE ADJACENT KITCHEN KEEPS THE COFFEE CUPS TOPPED.

—84

THE DINING ROOM OPENS ONTO THE GREAT ROOM, SO BOTH CAN BASK IN THE
WARMTH OF A ROARING FIRE.

THE FIRST FLOOR BEDROOM OVERLOOKS THE FRONT PORCH. A TROPHY ABOVE
THE BED AND EXPOSED FLOORBOARDS FROM ABOVE ADD TO THE RUSTIC CHARM.

The Ranch

Photography by Hayley Ferguson

FIRST FLOOR

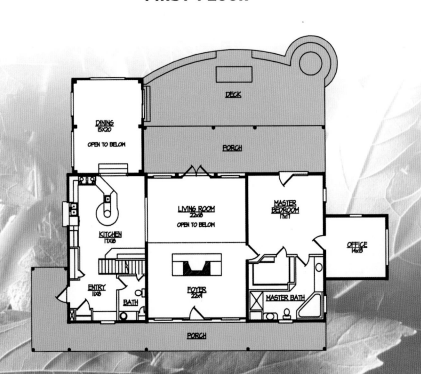

DINING
15x20
OPEN TO BELOW

DECK

PORCH

KITCHEN
11x18

LIVING ROOM
22x18
OPEN TO BELOW

MASTER
BEDROOM
17x17

OFFICE
14x15

ENTRY
11x8

FOYER
22x9

MASTER BATH

BATH

PORCH

SECOND FLOOR

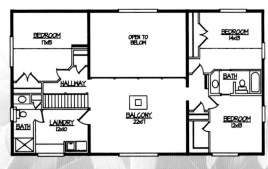

BEDROOM
11x15

OPEN TO BELOW

BEDROOM
14x19

HALLWAY

BATH

BATH

LAUNDRY
12x10

BALCONY
22x17

BEDROOM
12x13

THIRD FLOOR

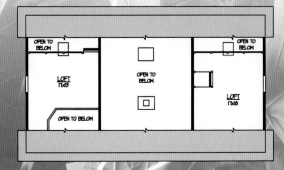

OPEN TO BELOW

OPEN TO BELOW

LOFT
11x15

OPEN TO BELOW

LOFT
11x18

OPEN TO BELOW

This is no simple two-story stretch of home; this is a paradise where every bit of space, indoors and out, has been crafted to suit the owner's sensibilities. Nothing was spared in planning a home that incorporated only the best — enormous timbers for the construction, fine woodwork, hand-cut stone, and ceramic tiles for the floors. Lofts occupy what would be attic space in mere mortal homes, and look down three stories on a living room that acts as the true hub of home. There are three bedrooms upstairs for the children, while the parents enjoy a master suite and a bump-out private office on the first floor. Outside the home, entire trees were used for picture-perfect porch supports, and branching out from there is impressive landscaping any gardener would be proud to lay claim to. Here is a home — named Giles Ranch — that anyone would be happy to post their name in front of.

ENTIRE TREES WERE USED TO BOLSTER UP A LONG STRETCH OF FRONT PORCH OVERHANG. RUSTIC ROCKERS AND LIGHTING COMPLETE WITH CEILING FANS MAKE THIS DECK AN INVITING REFUGE FROM SUN OR RAIN.

Photography by Harley Ferguson

AN OLD, PAINTED CAST-IRON GEAR FORMS THE HUB OF THE KITCHEN, CREATING A UNIQUE AND COLORFUL SEATING AREA. IMMACULATE WOODWORK PAIRS WITH EARTHY CERAMIC TILE FOR A GORGEOUS KITCHEN FLOOR. TRACK LIGHTING BETWEEN RAW WOOD BEAMS ENSURE A BRIGHT ATMOSPHERE, EVEN FOR MIDNIGHT SNACKS. A SEPARATE WING IS SET ASIDE FOR FORMAL DINING.

Photography by Harley Ferguson

91

Photography by Harley Ferguson

Photography by Harley Ferguson

Photography by Harley Ferguson

STEPPING UNDER MASSIVE LOG BEAMS, A VISITOR ENTERS A RUSTIC FRONT DOOR TO A STONE AND WOOD FOYER. THE STONE WALL THEY FACE IS ACTUALLY THE BACK OF AN ENORMOUS FIREPLACE THAT FRONTS THE LIVING ROOM.

Photography by Harley Ferguson

A LOFT IS DEFINED BY NATURAL WOOD RAILING OVERLOOKING AN IMPRESSIVE LIVING ROOM.
BESIDES A FREESTANDING FIREPLACE OF FIELDSTONE, THE LIVING ROOM IS ALSO ANCHORED
BY A CENTRAL RECTANGLE OF FLAGSTONE SURROUNDED BY AN ARTISTIC WOOD FLOOR. RUSTIC
ARTIFACTS WERE USED TO DECORATE THE ROOM, WHICH SOARS ALL THE WAY UP TO THE
THIRD-FLOOR RAFTERS.

Photography by Harley Ferguson

THE MASTER SUITE INCORPORATES THE SAME WOOD FLOOR ARTISTRY EXHIBITED THROUGHOUT THE FIRST FLOOR. A PRIVATE OFFICE IS ACCESSED ONLY VIA THE BEDROOM, MAKING IT A REFUGE FOR WORK AND CONTEMPLATION. IN THE MASTER BATH, A BRICK MASONRY SURROUND CONCEALS THE ULTRA-MODERN LUXURY OF A WHIRL-POOL TUB.

Photography by Harley Ferguson

95

Photography by Harley Ferguson

Photography by Harley Ferguson

THREE UPSTAIRS BEDROOMS ARE FURNISHED FOR THE CHILDREN,
WITH HEAVY RAFTERS EXPOSED TO HELP ABSORB A LOT OF NOISE.

Indoor/Outdoor Paradise

Taking a standard floor plan and packing it with pleasure, these homeowners set themselves up quite nicely. Inside, they've created an air-conditioned paradise from a sparkly entertainment room that's the envy of all to a cozy fire-lit master bedroom reserved for two. Outside they enjoy an above ground spa with a view over an all-natural swimming pool. A perfect piece of paradise.

99

TUCKED INTO THE WOODS, THE SITE WAS LEFT AS INTACT AS POSSIBLE WHEN THIS NEW LOG HOME WAS BUILT. THE OWNERS DID MAKE SOME MODIFICATIONS TO MOTHER NATURE, THOUGH, IN THE FORM OF A MAN-MADE POND AND AN ABOVE-GROUND SPA SET AMIDST CAREFULLY LANDSCAPED SUR-ROUNDINGS THAT PRESERVE THE LUSHNESS OF THE FOREST.

One Big Roof

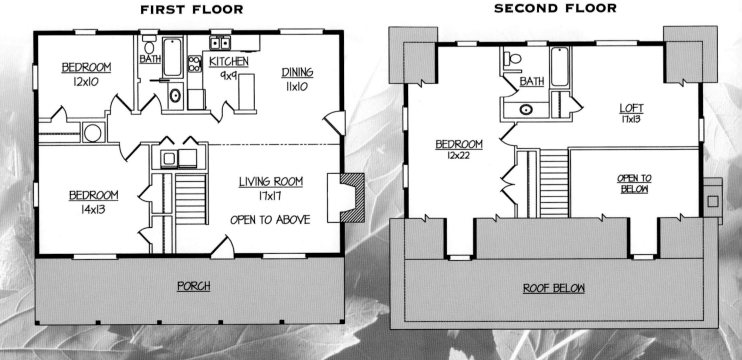

FIRST FLOOR

BEDROOM
12x10

BATH

KITCHEN
9x9

DINING
11x10

BEDROOM
14x13

LIVING ROOM
17x17

OPEN TO ABOVE

PORCH

SECOND FLOOR

BATH

LOFT
17x13

BEDROOM
12x22

OPEN TO
BELOW

ROOF BELOW

An enormous tin roof crowns this jewel of a log home in an idyllic country setting. Beneath the striking red and wood exterior, a simple arrangement of rooms provides an enormous amount of living space for a retired couple, with room for children and grandchildren to visit. Attired in handsome country style, the home is a virtual showplace of gracious country living.

F&E Schmidt Photography

BUCOLIC IN ITS APPEARANCE, THIS WONDERFUL HOME EPITOMIZES SIMPLE COUNTRY LIVING. A SECOND-FLOOR BUMP OUT HOUSES THE MASTER BED AND BATH, AND ADDS A SLIGHTLY ASYMMETRICAL APPEARANCE TO THE HOME.

RIVERSTONE SURROUNDS THE LIVING ROOM FIREPLACE, WHICH OPENS THROUGH THE SECOND STORY OF THE HOME. ANTIQUED CABINETRY CONCEALS THE TELEVISION AND SOUND SYSTEM IN THE CORNER, KEEPING WITH THE RUSTIC NATURE OF THE HOME.

F&E Schmidt Photography

TWO BEDROOMS OCCUPY ONE SIDE OF THE FIRST FLOOR. THIS ONE OPENS ONTO THE FRONT PORCH.

BEAD BOARD CABINETRY
IN THE KITCHEN WAS
GIVEN A FAINT BLUE
WASH, SETTING IT APART
FROM THE ENORMOUS
BEAMS AND PINE FLOOR-
ING. THE DINING ROOM
LOOKS OUT A SLIDING
GLASS DOOR TO A NEW
SCREENED-IN PORCH
ADDITION.

A SCREENED PORCH
AND DECK WERE LATER
ADDITIONS TO THE
HOME. BESIDES BRING-
ING THE OWNERS
CLOSER TO THE WOODS
BEYOND THEIR HOME,
THE ADDITION ALLOWS
THEM A VIEW OF THE
MATCHING BARN/
WORKSHOP.

MASTER BED AND BATH WERE TUCKED
UNDER THE EAVES. THE UPSTAIRS SUITE
IS AN EXPANSIVE ESCAPE, OCCUPYING
THE BETTER PART OF THE SECOND
FLOOR, WITH ROOM TO SPARE FOR AN
OVERLOOK TO THE LIVING ROOM.

F&E Schmidt Photography

FIRST FLOOR

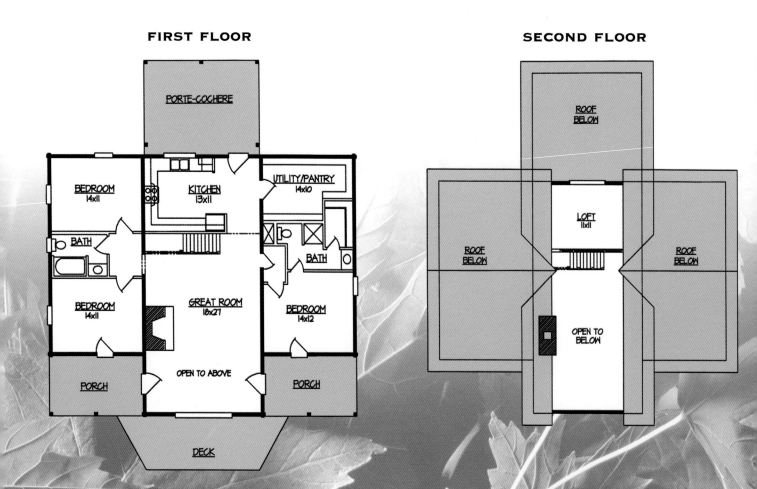

PORTE-COCHERE

BEDROOM
14x11

KITCHEN
13x11

UTILITY/PANTRY
14x10

BATH

BATH

BEDROOM
14x11

GREAT ROOM
18x27

BEDROOM
14x12

OPEN TO ABOVE

PORCH

PORCH

DECK

SECOND FLOOR

ROOF
BELOW

LOFT
11x11

ROOF
BELOW

ROOF
BELOW

OPEN TO
BELOW

A weekend getaway, this log bunkhouse is full of aesthetic surprises. Bedrooms hug the outside walls, while the interior is devoted to a soaring space for dining and hanging out by the fire. The kitchen is tucked under a loft area, which doubles as a fourth bedroom when needed. The approach to the home is characterized by a car shelter. The back is devoted to outdoor living space — two covered porches, a deck, and a wall of windows overlooking the wilderness.

A COMPACT WEEKEND CABIN BELIES THE LUXURY TO BE FOUND WITHIN.

DINING AND LIVING ARES ARE UNDER AN INSPIRING CATHEDRAL
CEILING. AN ANTLER CHANDELIER CASTS A WARM GLOW ON LATE-
NIGHT GHOST OR HUNTING STORIES. A BOOKCASE OFFERS
INVITING READS SHOULD COMPANY AND WEATHER FAIL.

111—

Because grand gatherings with friends and family was the whole point, the home was furnished with ample beds and bedding.

Kitchen, dining, and living areas seamlessly flow into each other. A screened porch beyond the dining area is a favorite spot when the weather agrees. The kitchen and dining area enjoy added headroom under open eaves.

115—

A FOYER CREATES AN OPEN-AIR PASSAGEWAY BETWEEN KITCHEN, LIVING ROOM, AND A DEN THAT DOUBLES AS A GUEST ROOM.

THE MASTER BEDROOM AND A GUEST ROOM
OCCUPY THE SECOND FLOOR, WHERE THE
EXPOSED LOGS AND CHINKING ARE EVERYWHERE
EVIDENT.

117—

Living Large

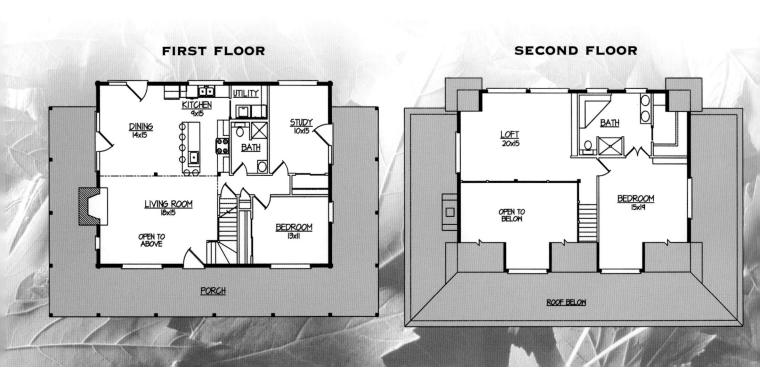

FIRST FLOOR

DINING
14x15

KITCHEN
9x15

UTILITY

STUDY
10x15

BATH

LIVING ROOM
18x15

OPEN TO
ABOVE

BEDROOM
13x11

PORCH

SECOND FLOOR

LOFT
20x15

BATH

OPEN TO
BELOW

BEDROOM
15x19

ROOF BELOW

This home was designed around enormous living spaces, including a study that would inspire anyone's work. A roof overhang also allows for a wonderful wrap-around porch on the first floor, elevated above a walk-out basement. The home design is packed with visual variety and space-expanding advantages. The end result is a palatial, rural retreat.

Harley Ferguson Photography

FROM THE FRONT, THIS HOME APPEARS TO BE A HUMBLE LOG CABIN, COMPLETE WITH AN INVITING PORCH AND TOPPED BY DORMERS. IN BACK, HOWEVER, IT SOARS UP FROM THE SLOPING LOT, WITH A STONE CHIMNEY TOWERING THREE-STORIES HIGH.

A LOFTY VIEW DRAMATICALLY ILLUSTRATES THE SOARING CAPABILITIES OF
GIRDERS AND OVERHEAD BEAMS. MASSIVE BEAMS ALSO SERVE AS AN EXCELLENT
VEHICLE FOR TRACK LIGHTING. A LOG WALL BACKS THE STONE FIREPLACE,
PROVIDING A DRAMATIC BACKDROP FOR THIS BRIGHT, OPEN ROOM.

OPPOSITE PAGE:

AN OPEN KITCHEN/DINING AREA PROVIDES
SEATING BOTH AT THE COUNTERTOP OR THE
ADJACENT TABLE. EXPOSED GIRDERS AND
OVERHEAD BEAMS OPEN THE HEADSPACE
IN THE GREAT ROOM.

—122

AN ENORMOUS LOFT AREA IS A WONDERFUL RETREAT, WITH BIRD'S-EYE VIEW
WINDOWS THAT SHED PLENTY OF LIGHT ON A GOOD BOOK.

123

THE MASTER BEDROOM IS TUCKED UP UNDER THE EAVES, WITH A
DORMER CREATING ADDITIONAL ARCHITECTURAL INTEREST.

Pleasure Palace

FIRST FLOOR

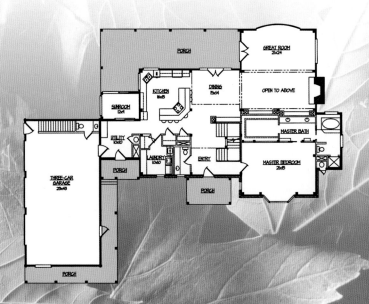

SECOND FLOOR

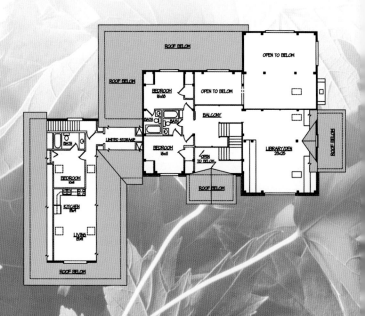

Built by a big family, this home was designed to be lived and played in. Lots of recreational space was built into the plan, with a great room, plus a sunroom and a lofty game room. Not to mention a wonderful covered porch and and covered patio in back. Even an in-law/guest suite was including over the garage — with a separate kitchen, living, bedroom, and bath provided – to provide room for friends and visiting family.

DEDICATED TO LIFE'S PLEASURES, THIS HOME AFFORDS FAMILY MEMBERS LOTS OF LIVING SPACE, INDOORS AND OUT.
THE LOFTY TIMBER FRAME STRUCTURE WAS SET ATOP A HANDSOME STONE FOUNDATION.

STACKING THE WALL WITH CABINETRY AND PROVIDING PANTRY SPACE IN AN ADJACENT LAUNDRY ROOM, THE HOMEOWNERS WERE ABLE TO KEEP THEIR KITCHEN OPEN, WITH A COMMANDING VIEW OF THE DINING ROOM AND THE HOME ENTRYWAY. BAR STOOLS AT THE TWO ISLANDS MAKE THE KITCHEN A HANGOUT.

THE GREAT ROOM INCLUDES A WET BAR WITH AN UNDER-COUNTER REFRIGERATOR TO SAVE ON TRIPS TO THE KITCHEN.

OVERLOOKING THE GREAT ROOM, A LOFT HAS BEEN UTILIZED AS A GAMING CENTER, WITH A POOL TABLE AND A CARD TABLE FOR ENTERTAINMENT. AGAIN, A FULLY-STOCKED WET BAR IS READY FOR LIBATIONS AND REFRESHMENTS, MINIMIZING THE NEED TO GO DOWNSTAIRS.

A BOW WINDOW CHARACTERIZES THE MASTER BEDROOM, WHERE COMFORTABLE CHAIRS AND A TABLE ARE AT THE READY FOR A PRIVATE CHAT OR MORNING COFFEE.

TWO BEDROOMS ARE TUCKED UNDER THE EAVES UPSTAIRS, WITH SEPARATE BATHS.

Rob Franzese Photography

FIRST FLOOR

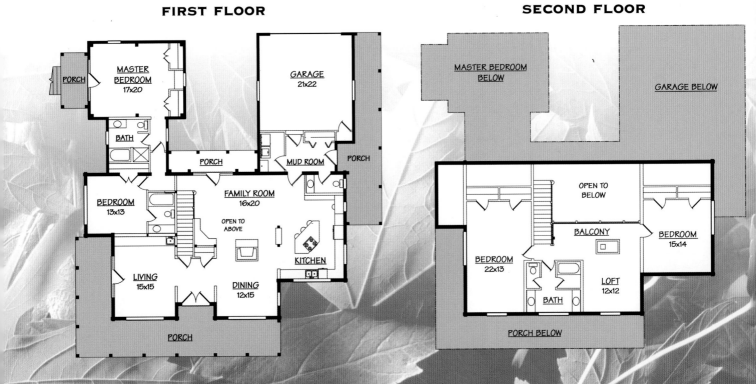

PORCH

MASTER BEDROOM 17x20

BATH

PORCH

BEDROOM 13x13

FAMILY ROOM 16x20

OPEN TO ABOVE

LIVING 15x15

DINING 12x15

KITCHEN

PORCH

GARAGE 21x22

MUD ROOM

PORCH

SECOND FLOOR

MASTER BEDROOM BELOW

GARAGE BELOW

OPEN TO BELOW

BEDROOM 22x13

BALCONY

BEDROOM 15x14

BATH

LOFT 12x12

PORCH BELOW

In designing their home, these owners put their rooms where they wanted them, rejecting a four-sided mentality. The result is a home that flows according to their needs inside, and that presents a fascinating study in varied rooflines and façade. The layout of the home takes a traditional, Colonial approach on first entry – with a living room and dining room just off the entry foyer. Beyond that, though, they've mixed things up a bit. Family members actually enter through the back, from a garage separated from the house by a covered porch and an enclosed entry with an air lock. A master bedroom has its own wing and private porch. The two children sleep upstairs, separated by a balcony.

Bob Franzese Photography

THE FIRST FLOOR OF THIS HOME WAS BUILT FROM LOGS WHILE THE SECOND STORY SOARS ON TIMBER FRAME. THE HOME WAS SET AMIDST ROLLING MOUNTAINS, AND WINDOWS AND PORCHES TAKE FULL ADVANTAGE OF THE VIEW.

Bob Franzese Photography

ALTHOUGH CALLED THE DINING ROOM, THE FAMILY ESCHEWED FORMAL DESIGN, PICKING ECLECTIC FURNISHINGS TO COMPLEMENT THE LOG CONSTRUCTION.

—132

A CATHEDRAL CEILING IN THE FAMILY ROOM FOLLOWS THE STAIRS UP TO THE CHILDREN'S SLEEPING QUARTERS.

Bob Franzese Photography

THE DINING ROOM
WAS SET OFF BY
ITSELF, GIVING IT A
MORE FORMAL AIR,
WHILE THE KITCHEN
OPENS TOWARD THE
FAMILY ROOM.

133

Bob Franzese Photography

THE MASTER BEDROOM OPENS TO A PORCH AND A VISTA BEYOND THAT INVITES ONE OUT FOR A MORNING STROLL.

135—

THE CHILDREN ARE COMFORTABLY TUCKED AWAY UPSTAIRS, WHERE VAULTED CEILINGS AND THEIR OWN LOFTY BALCONY INSPIRE DREAMS AND GAMES OF MAKE-BELIEVE.

Bob Franzese Photography

Civil War Style

F&E Schmidt Photography

In realizing a long-time dream of living in a log cabin and opening a bed and breakfast, this couple had to give up on restoring an original log cabin. Instead, they selected a Civil War era style of log home design created by folk artist Bob Timberlake™ and licensed to Hearthstone. Thick strips of chinking follow the natural taper and shape of trees in uneven logs, creating a rustic appearance. Their home design follows a traditional courtyard plan in a giant square, though the courtyard is replaced by with a four-season great room, overlooked by balconies on the second floor. The homeowners have a master bedroom on one side of the second floor, with guest rooms circling the upstairs. A bonus room attached by a covered walkway acts as a special honeymoon suite.

F&E Schmidt Photography

DORMER WINDOWS ADD LIGHT TO UPSTAIRS BEDROOMS AND THE CENTRAL BALCONY. PORCH POSTS COMPLETE WITH LIMBS AND TWIGS CONTRIBUTE CHARACTER TO THE FAÇADE.

BECAUSE THE KITCHEN IS NOT A PUBLIC GATHERING PLACE IT WAS WALLED OFF FROM PUBLIC ACCESS AS A SEPARATE CHEF'S DOMAIN. NONETHE-LESS, THE OWNERS KEPT THE HISTORIC CHARM CLOSE AT HAND, INSTALLING A PERIOD-REPRODUCTION OVEN/ RANGE AND STICKING WITH THE HOME'S PERVASIVE USE OF WOODWORK. ADDITION-ALLY, THEY ADDED A SMALL BREAKFAST ROOM WHERE THEY CAN EAT SEPARATELY FROM THEIR GUESTS.

GUESTS ENJOY THE OWNERS' SPECIALTY EGG, CHEESE, AND
BACON PIE IN THE DINING ROOM.

BUILT-IN BOOKSHELVES
IN THE LIBRARY OFFER
CONTEMPLATIVE
ENTERTAINMENTS,
WHILE ACROSS A
SEATING AREA IS A
SMALL GAME ROOM.

THE BEDROOMS ARE ALL CHARMINGLY APPOINTED, WITH CIVIL WAR ERA APPROPRIATE ANTIQUES AND TEXTILES.

141—

Artist's Inspiration

F&E Schmidt Photography

A professional photographer, this artist was very exacting in their home designs. She wanted her favorite medium in excess upstairs – light. Plus a lower floor where she could tuck away a darkroom. Her partner liked the tradition and feel of log home construction, and both felt that a more traditional building style would suit their collection of antique furnishings. Together they achieved their goals by combining log with timber framing for a soaring, three-story home that extends up into a glorious third-floor loft.

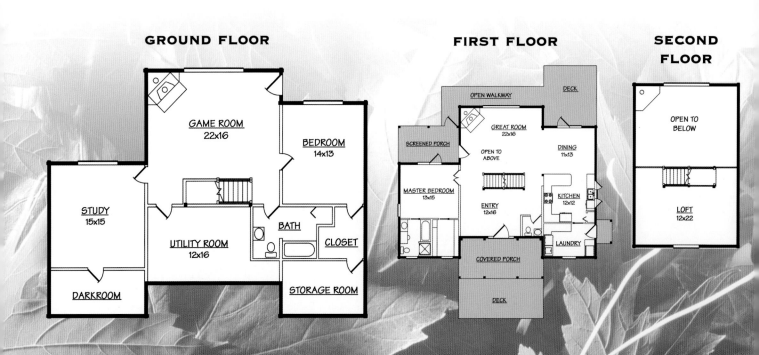

GROUND FLOOR

GAME ROOM
22x16

BEDROOM
14x13

STUDY
15x15

BATH

CLOSET

UTILITY ROOM
12x16

DARKROOM

STORAGE ROOM

FIRST FLOOR

OPEN WALKWAY

DECK

SCREENED PORCH

GREAT ROOM
22x16

OPEN TO
ABOVE

DINING
11x13

MASTER BEDROOM
13x15

KITCHEN
12x12

ENTRY
12x16

LAUNDRY

COVERED PORCH

DECK

SECOND FLOOR

OPEN TO
BELOW

LOFT
12x22

A GRAY FINISH ON THE ROUGH-HEWN EXTERIOR OF THIS LOG HOME GIVES IT AN AGED LOOK, THOUGH THE SOARING WALL OF WINDOWS ON THE BACKSIDE IS A DEAD GIVEAWAY TO ITS YOUTH. COVERED PORCHES AND LOTS OF DECKING ADD TO THE RURAL APPEAL OF THE HOMESITE.

—144

THE ENTRYWAY OPENS INTO A GRAND VIEW,
PAST THE OPEN-RAIL STAIRWAY AND INTO THE
GREAT ROOM BEYOND. THE DOORWAY ITSELF IS
DELICATE WITHIN THE MASSIVE LOGS THAT FLANK
IT, A HAND-CRAFTED STAINED GLASS OVAL SET IN
THE DOOR BETWEEN MATCHING SIDELIGHTS.

A WALL OF WINDOWS CHARAC-
TERIZES THE GREAT ROOM,
WHERE LOGS AND TIMBERS
CLIMB THREE STORIES INTO THE
AIR. RATHER THAN A FIREPLACE,
THE OWNERS OPTED FOR A
TRADITIONAL WOODSTOVE, WHICH
PULLS ITS WEIGHT IN PROVIDING
WINTER HEATING VALUE FOR THIS
MASSIVE ROOM.

146

Drywall finish and white appliances add contrast to a kitchen rich in wood.
A butcher block island is in perfect keeping with the architecture.

ANTIQUE TABLEWARE AND LINENS ARE PROUDLY SET OUT IN THE DINING ROOM. AN ANTIQUE SIDEBOARD FEELS RIGHT AT HOME UNDER A PORTRAIT HUNG ON THE EXPOSED LOG WALL.

THE MASTER BEDROOM OPENS TO A PRIVATE, SCREENED-IN PORCH.

F&E Schmidt Photography

A LOFTY, THIRD-FLOOR BEDROOM PUTS GUESTS AT THE TOP OF THE WORLD,
SITUATED AMONG THE RAFTERS AND NEXT TO A BREATHTAKING VIEW.

Winged Addition

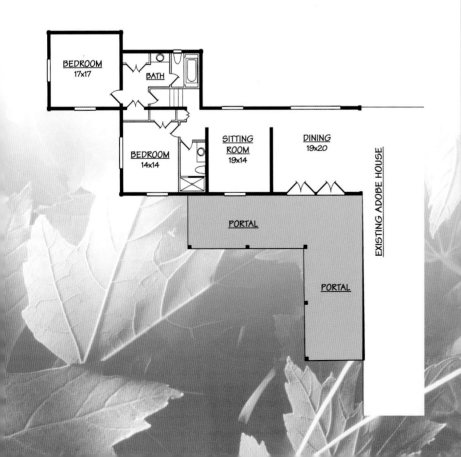

A COVERED COURTYARD CONNECTS ORIGINAL ADOBE
HOME WITH TWO STRETCHES OF LOG ADDITION.

BEDROOM
17x17

BATH

BEDROOM
14x14

SITTING ROOM
19x14

DINING
19x20

PORTAL

PORTAL

EXISTING ADOBE HOUSE

When it came time for a growing family to add bedrooms and additional living space, they wanted logs beside their adobe desert home. The two work together beautifully in a flowing ranch that looks like it dates back to the 1800s. There's a special alchemy between the architectural mediums, both growing out of the earth itself.

Harley Ferguson Photography

151—

THE ORIGINAL KITCHEN, COMPLETE WITH
BEAMED WOODEN CEILING, OPENS OUT TO
AN EXPANSIVE NEW DINING AREA COM-
PLETE WITH STONE FIREPLACE AND
CATHEDRAL CEILING.

WITHIN THE OLD ADOBE HOME, ONE SEES HOW LOGS WERE USED TO SUPPORT THE CEILING. ADOBE WALLS ACCOMMODATE WONDERFUL CURVES AND BUILT-IN FIREPLACES IN DISTINCT SOUTHWESTERN STYLE.

Harley Ferguson Photography

—154

A NEW SITTING ROOM OFFERS A
PLACE TO DIGEST A BIG MEAL,
JUST BEYOND THE DINING ROOM.
BOTH ROOMS OPEN TO A COV-
ERED PORCH THAT ACTS AS
PORTAL BETWEEN THE NEW AND
THE OLD IN THIS HOME.

Harley Ferguson Photography

Harley Ferguson Photography

TWO ADDITIONAL
BEDROOMS WERE
FURNISHED WITH
SOUTHWESTERN
STICK FURNISH-
INGS AND NATIVE-
PATTERN
BEDCOVERS.

155—

Bricks and Sticks

Don Kerkhof Photography

BRICK UNDERLINES A TIMBER FRAME HOME, ADDING A COLORFUL
UNDERLINE TO A MASSIVE STRUCTURE.

FIRST FLOOR

NOOK
9x12

KITCHEN
12x13

DINING
20x13

WINTER
ROOM
28x10

LIVING ROOM
30x16

SCREENED
PORCH

DEN
16x14

OPEN TO
BELOW

SECOND FLOOR

COVERED
PORCH

BATH

MASTER
BEDROOM
15x24

PORCH

OPEN TO
BELOW

LAUNDRY

BALCONY

BEDROOM
14x13

BALCONY

BEDROOM
17x14

BEDROOM
12x22

Timber framing was used to create a home that adds elevation to an amazing hilltop lot. In building their dream home, the owners spared no expense or space. The result is a dream castle. Downstairs the family enjoys all the expected amenities of a home. When it comes to mealtime, they have their choice between the formal dining room, a breakfast nook, or a screened in porch – all off the open kitchen. Upstairs, the four bedrooms branch off a central hallway, and all have access to a balcony that communicates with the great room downstairs, or opens to the outdoors for a magnificent second-floor view. The master of the house has a private den off the front entryway where he can meet with clients without disturbing family life within.

Don Kerkhof Photography

Don Kerkhof Photography

—158—

EXACTING WORK WITH HEAVY TIMBERS ALLOWS HOME SPACES TO TOWER. THE
EFFECT OF FINISHED DRYWALL AND THE ENORMOUS, EXPOSED BEAMS IS
BREATHTAKING.

THE LIVING ROOM SITS UNDER A CATHEDRAL CEILING. FRENCH DOORS OPEN TO
AN ENCLOSED SUNROOM BEYOND, A PERFECT PLACE TO BASK IN WINTER'S
SUNLIGHT. TILE FLOORING AND THE BRICK-BACK TO THE FIREPLACE ADD CHARAC-
TER TO THIS "WINTER ROOM".

ABOVE AND OPPOSITE PAGE, TOP:

TILE UNIFIES THE KITCHEN WITH THE NEARBY BREAKFAST NOOK. A CENTRAL FIREPLACE UNIT SHEDS WARM LIGHT ON THE INTERIOR.

Don Kerkhof Photography

THE MASTER BEDROOM OPENS TO A
PRIVATE, COVERED PORCH ON THE
BACKSIDE OF THE HOME.

Don Kerkhof Photography

A GREEN ROOF ALLOWS THIS LOG HOME TO SHIMMER BACK AT THE LAKE.

H&E Schmidt Photography

FIRST FLOOR

SECOND FLOOR

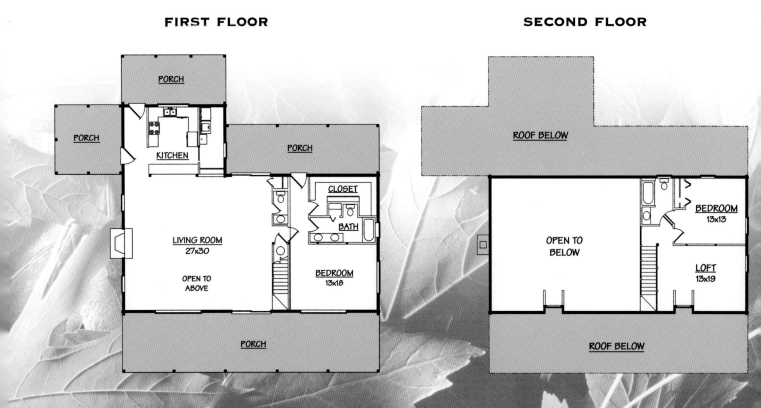

First Floor
- PORCH
- PORCH
- PORCH
- KITCHEN
- CLOSET
- BATH
- LIVING ROOM
  27x30
- OPEN TO ABOVE
- BEDROOM
  13x18
- PORCH

Second Floor
- ROOF BELOW
- OPEN TO BELOW
- BEDROOM
  13x13
- LOFT
  13x19
- ROOF BELOW

Porches are the most prominent feature of this compact weekend home. Built on a hillside with a commanding view of the lake beyond, the house is flanked front and rear by covered porches. In planning their vacation home, the owners didn't worry about incorporating a dining room – the goal was to be outside whenever the weather permitted. Of course, there's a contingency plan, should Mother Nature be undergoing a particularly bad hair day – a foldout table where dinner might be taken. Further, the living room is ample and inviting, with a fireplace and a cathedral ceiling that would lure most people to gather here.

Bold by design, these homeowners stuck with simple, classics and antiques for their furnishings. The result is a perfect complement to two stories of log wall in the living room.

167—

ABOVE AND OPPOSITE PAGE, BOTTOM:

Two bedrooms with full baths were designed for the house.

Red Roof In

F&E Schmidt Photography

A wonderful tin roof caps this log and timber-frame hybrid, where the beauty of log walls is crowned in a central great room, framed by soaring beams. A second floor deck traces the back of the log home, creating a viewing platform that is an irresistible draw for the occupants of this hilltop home. Inside, nature's best has been used in the construction, from the wood logs and framing to the stone floors, chimneys, and support columns. Most importantly, the homeowners custom designed their house to incorporate lots of light, splashed throughout the central part of the home via huge picture windows, and filtered into cozy wings by an open floor plan.

A GENEROUS EXPANSE OF CIRCULAR DRIVE BRINGS ONE TO THE FRONT OF THIS HOME, WHICH APPEARS TO BE A LONG STRETCH OF RANCH. IN THE BACK, HOWEVER, ONE FINDS THEMSELVES CHOOSING BETWEEN GROUND-LEVEL LIVING AREAS, AND A SECOND FLOOR THAT CLIMBS TO CATHEDRAL HEIGHTS.

F&E Schmidt Photography

Facing the street, the great room is secreted behind a stone chimney, with windows high up that let in lots of light, but no curious looks. On the backside of the house, it's all glass.

A FOYER ADMITS ONE
TO THE DELIGHTS OF
THE HOME — EXPOSED
BEAMS AND LOG WALLS,
STONE FLOOR, AND
ANTIQUE FURNISHINGS.

BLACK STAIN ON THE
KITCHEN CABINETRY ADDS
CONTRAST TO THE WOOD
SURROUNDINGS, AND IS IN
KEEPING WITH THE TRADI-
TIONAL FURNISHINGS.

A DINING AREA DOUBLES AS LIBRARY, WITH SHELVING TAKING ADVANTAGE OF A TALL WALL TO HOUSE A HOST OF FAVORITE READING MATERIAL. STONE CHIMNEYS FLANK TWO SIDES OF THE ROOM, WITH ONE OFFERING A FIRE-PLACE TO DINERS.

F&E Schmidt Photography

THE MASTERS OF THE
HOUSE DIDN'T STINT ON
SPACE — FLOOR OR
CEILING — WHEN THEY
CREATED THEIR SUITE.

173

F&E Schmidt Photography

Folks Home

FIRST FLOOR

GARAGE
39x24

PORCH

SUN ROOM
19x11

LIVING ROOM
34x16

OFFICE
10x13

KITCHEN
10x16

FOYER

DINING
11x16

UTILITY
14x11

PORCH

SECOND FLOOR

ATTIC

STORAGE
40x12

ATTIC

ROOF BELOW

MASTER BATH

BATH

BEDROOM
13x15

ROOF BELOW

MASTER BEDROOM
16x14

SITTING
6x11

BEDROOM
14x15

ROOF BELOW

ROOF BELOW

Harley Ferguson Photography

A desire for tradition led these homeowners to a mixture of stone, log, and timber frame construction – a perfect framework for a collection of folk arts. Their home follows a traditional plan, as well, with a Colonial center hall design, the bedrooms stacked upstairs. The family uses a back garage entrance that opens into a utility room. Storage space was built in above the garage, allowing more space in the home to be left open. Living spaces include an enormous stretch of living room, a sunroom, and a sitting area upstairs.

PORCHES FRONT AND BACK ARE WONDERFUL DRAWS ALONG THE FRONT AND BACK STRETCHES OF THIS LOG AND STONE HOME.

A FOYER AREA LEADS BACK TO A PRIVATE OFFICE. IN TYPICAL COLONIAL LAYOUT, THERE IS A DINING ROOM TO THE RIGHT, A LIVING ROOM TO THE LEFT.

A FIREPLACE IS A WARM ADDITION TO ANY MEAL, AND ACTS AS DIVIDER BETWEEN DINING ROOM AND KITCHEN.

A LONG STRETCH OF LIVING ROOM AND AN ADJACENT SUNROOM ARE TWO POPULAR FAMILY HANGOUTS.

177

TWO UPSTAIRS BEDROOMS ENJOY BOW-FRONT WINDOWS WITH SPECTACULAR VIEWS. ONE IS USED AS A SITTING AREA.

F&E Schmidt Photography

This is a stunning example of a small log cabin made perfect. The artwork, the furnishings, and the simple straightforward design of the structure itself speak perfection for those who dream of log cabin living. Deceptively small in appearance from outside, this is a three-bedroom home with three full baths. Everything about this home, including the lot, speaks charm, all-American style.

FIRST FLOOR

SECOND FLOOR

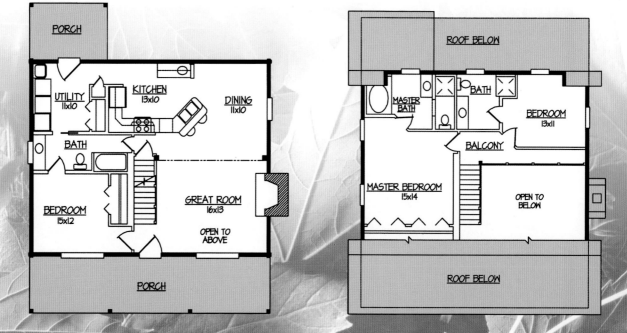

PORCH

UTILITY
11x10

KITCHEN
13x10

DINING
11x10

BATH

BEDROOM
15x12

GREAT ROOM
16x13

OPEN TO
ABOVE

PORCH

ROOF BELOW

BATH

MASTER
BATH

BEDROOM
13x11

BALCONY

MASTER BEDROOM
15x14

OPEN TO
BELOW

ROOF BELOW

FROM THE PERFECTLY TENDED GROUNDS TO THE PERFECT LOG CABIN SET BACK AGAINST THE TREES, YOU MIGHT THINK YOU'D STEPPED INTO A TREASURED PROPERTY ON THE NATIONAL HISTORIC REGISTER. IT'S ALL NEW, HOWEVER, BUT NO LESS TREASURED.

—180

A GREAT ROOM IS THE FIRST TO GREET VISITORS WHEN THEY ENTER THE FRONT DOOR.
BESIDES HANDSOME LOG WALLS THAT SOAR ABOVE A STONE FIREPLACE TO A CATHEDRAL
CEILING, THEY ARE GREETED BY A HANDSOME COLLECTION OF FOLK/AMERICANA ARTWORK.
A COLLECTION OF ROOSTER ART SETS THE THEME.

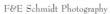

THE KITCHEN AND DINING AREAS ARE SIMPLY FURNISHED IN A BLUE AND WHITE MOTIF, CLASSIC COUNTRY STYLE.

MASTER BED AND BATH WERE TUCKED UP UNDER THE EAVES. A WALLPAPER MOTIF WAS CAREFULLY HAND-PAINTED ONTO THE CLAW-FOOT TUB TO CREATE A UNIFORM LOOK THROUGHOUT.

Porch Rich

Poised on the verge of outdoors, these homeowners designed their home as a place where they retreat when the weather turns sour. Front and back porches and a deck are constant draws. Not that the inside is shabby. Rather, the warm log-lined interior is furnished comfortably and decorated artfully with antiques and sentimental pieces, creating a true family environment.

183—

A LOW-LYING LOG HOME BLENDS WITH THE FORESTED SURROUNDINGS.

A HAMMOCK BECKONS IN ONE CORNER OF A LONG, SCREENED-IN PORCH. HOWEVER, IT'S UNLIKELY THAT THE USER WILL BE ALONE LONG. THIS IS A FAMILY DRAWN TO THE OUTDOORS.

THE FRONT DOOR OPENS DIRECTLY
INTO AN IMPRESSIVE FAMILY ROOM,
DOMINATED BY A DOUBLE-WIDE
FIREPLACE SET IN A MASSIVE STONE
CHIMNEY.

Roger Wade Photography

AN ISLAND COOKTOP PUTS THE CHEF IN DIRECT CONTACT WITH HER FAMILY IN THE DINING AREA BEYOND.

MOM AND DAD NESTLE DOWN UNDER A LOFTY CATHEDRAL CEILING.

Roger Wade Photography

Wide Open Spaces

Don Kerkhof Photography

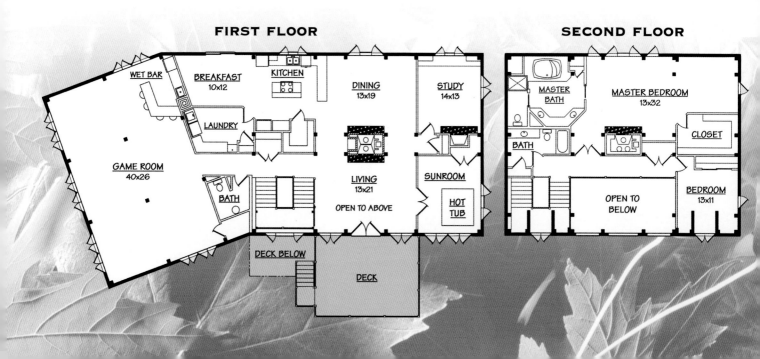

FIRST FLOOR

WET BAR

BREAKFAST
10x12

KITCHEN

DINING
13x19

STUDY
14x13

LAUNDRY

GAME ROOM
40x26

BATH

LIVING
13x21

OPEN TO ABOVE

SUNROOM

HOT
TUB

DECK BELOW

DECK

SECOND FLOOR

MASTER
BATH

MASTER BEDROOM
13x32

CLOSET

BATH

OPEN TO
BELOW

BEDROOM
13x11

The great advantages of timber frame construction lie in the ability to create vast, open rooms and amazing window areas. These proud homeowners were all about space when they designed a three-story home. It builds up from an enormous, above-ground basement —housing three cars, a workshop, a guest bedroom, a family room with fireplace, and a lot of storage and mechanical space — to a third story with a complete master suite, a children's room, and an exciting balcony overlooking the first-floor living room. All in all, an enormous, gracious space in which to dwell.

189

IN A WORD, THIS HOUSE IS IMPRESSIVE, BOTH IN TERMS OF SIZE AND NUMBER OF WINDOWS. THE OWNERS USED TIMBER FRAME CONSTRUCTION TO GIVE THEMSELVES PLENTY OF SPACE IN WHICH TO WORK AND PLAY.

—190

Sightlines between kitchen, dining, and living areas are afforded by massive support beams that make interior walls unnecessary. A central stone fireplace sheds heat and light to both dining and living rooms, and provides a decorative barrier.

191—

NATURAL WOOD AND CREAM TONES ADD INTIMACY TO A LARGE KITCHEN.

Long-Term Plans

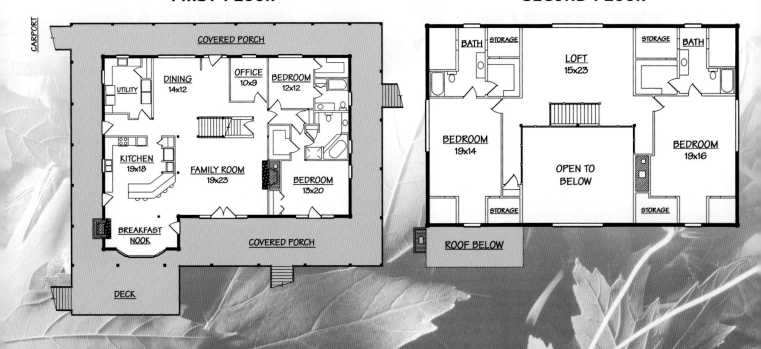

F&E Schmidt Photography

FIRST FLOOR

CARPORT

COVERED PORCH

UTILITY

DINING
14x12

OFFICE
10x9

BEDROOM
12x12

KITCHEN
19x18

FAMILY ROOM
19x23

BEDROOM
13x20

BREAKFAST
NOOK

COVERED PORCH

DECK

SECOND FLOOR

BATH

STORAGE

STORAGE

BATH

LOFT
15x23

BEDROOM
19x14

OPEN TO
BELOW

BEDROOM
19x16

STORAGE

STORAGE

ROOF BELOW

In planning a retirement, you want to take into account how your needs might change. You might not want to, or might not be able to, climb those stairs. And you don't want to have to carry those groceries so far from the car to the kitchen. And you probably will want to sit out on the porch in a rocker. So these homeowners planned ahead. They put the master bedroom on the first floor, and provided spacious bedrooms for the kids upstairs. They forked their driveway, allowing for a branch that led straight to a carport, and a covered porch walk to the first floor. Plus, they provided themselves with plenty of porch – wrapping almost the entire home in comfortable, rocker-friendly boards. The result is a perfect home for a maturing family.

193

F&E Schmidt Photography

A LOG HOME PRESENTS A LONG FACE TO ARRIVING GUESTS, WITH A DORMER-VARIED
ROOFLINE. IN BACK, THE HOME SWEEPS OUT OVER A WALK-OUT BASEMENT, CREATING A
BACKYARD HABITAT AT ONE WITH THE WOODED HILLSIDE.

—194

THE KITCHEN IS FLANKED ON EITHER SIDE BY A DINING ROOM AND A BREAKFAST NOOK — BOTH WITH COMMANDING VIEWS OUTDOORS. HOWEVER, ONLY THE FAMILY'S EATING NOOK INCLUDES A VIEW INTO THE CHEF.

THE LIVING ROOM IS FLOODED WITH FOREST-FILTERED SUNLIGHT. AN ENTIRE WALL OF GLASS DOORS OPENS ONTO THAT RETIREMENT PLAN — ROCKERS ON THE PORCH BEYOND.

195

THE FIRST-FLOOR MASTER BEDROOM OPENS ONTO A COVERED PORCH.

All Decked Out

Porches and deck flank front, back and one side of this comfortable, two-story log home. Inside, the owners enjoy a spectacular living room/kitchen area in an interior characterized by open spaces. Two guest rooms were provided upstairs to encourage frequent family visits.

FIRST FLOOR

SECOND FLOOR

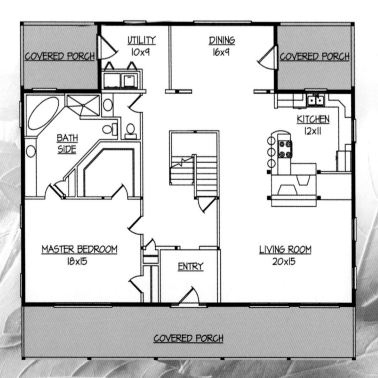

COVERED PORCH

UTILITY
10x9

DINING
16x9

COVERED PORCH

BATH
SIDE

KITCHEN
12x11

MASTER BEDROOM
18x15

ENTRY

LIVING ROOM
20x15

COVERED PORCH

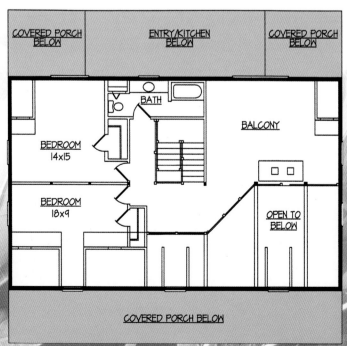

COVERED PORCH
BELOW

ENTRY/KITCHEN
BELOW

COVERED PORCH
BELOW

BATH

BALCONY

BEDROOM
14x15

BEDROOM
18x9

OPEN TO
BELOW

COVERED PORCH BELOW

A LOG HOME RISES TWO STORIES,
FLANKED BY SPACIOUS PORCHES AND
DECK AND SHADED BY A DOUBLE
ROOF OVERHANG.

199—

A SPACIOUS KITCHEN REVOLVES
AROUND AN ANTIQUE BUTCHER-BLOCK
TABLE. THE OUTSIDE WALL IS AN
ISLAND EATING COUNTER, AND PRO-
VIDES AN OVERLOOK FOR THE CHEF
INTO THE DINING AND LIVING ROOM
AREAS. THE ORIGINAL PLANS CALLED
FOR A FIREPLACE WITH ONE FACE INTO
THE KITCHEN, ANOTHER INTO THE
LIVING ROOM. BUT THESE WERE
MODIFIED, MOVING THE CHIMNEY TO
AN OUTSIDE LIVING ROOM WALL TO
OPEN THE VIEW.

—200

COMFORTABLE CRAFTSMAN-STYLE SEATING
AND A WARM FIRE DRAW THE FAMILY INTO THE
LIVING ROOM AT THE FRONT OF THE HOME.

201—

A FIRST-FLOOR MASTER SUITE EMPLOYS PRIVACY, SHELTERED FROM THE LIVING AREAS BY THE CENTRAL STAIRCASE. A SPACIOUS BATH, CLOSET, AND AMPLE ROOM ASSURE EASE AND ACCESSIBILITY.

203—

UPSTAIRS THERE IS A LOFT SEATING AREA WITH A STUPENDOUS VIEW OF THE LIVING ROOM BELOW. TWO BEDROOMS ARE SET UP FOR A VISITING CHILD AND THE GRANDCHILDREN.

Photography by Don Kerkhof

THE QUAINT
KITCHEN IS
EQUIPPED WITH A
CENTRAL ISLAND,
AND IS COMBINED
WITH THE DINING
ROOM FOR INTIMATE
ENTERTAINING.

206

Photography by Don Kerkhof

207—

THE LIVING ROOM IS SPACIOUS WITH A HEAVY TIMBER CATHEDRAL ROOF SYSTEM, GRAND FIREPLACE, AND ACCESS TO BOTH PORCHES.

Garden Party

This forest home has warm, sun-filled rooms, a lovely screened-in porch with a view of the gardens, an additional deck and patio for lazy, sunny afternoons, and a spacious two car garage to store the toys. Inside, the masters of the house enjoy a private wing, with walk-in closets, a huge soaking tub, and ample room for a king-size bed. An enormous living room, kitchen and dining area anchor the soaring, central part of the home, overlooked by a loft that serves as guest room when there are visitors.

FIRST FLOOR

SECOND FLOOR

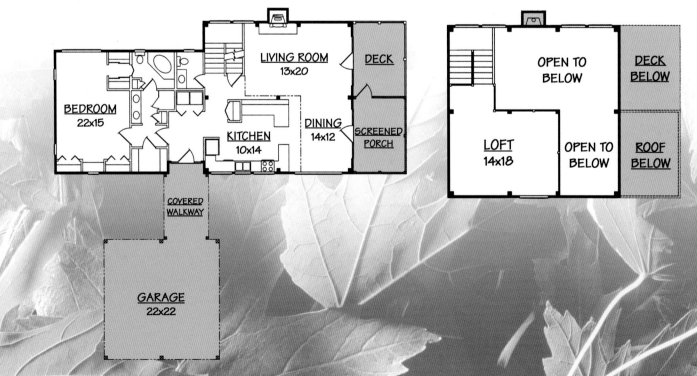

FIRST FLOOR:
- BEDROOM 22x15
- LIVING ROOM 13x20
- DECK
- KITCHEN 10x14
- DINING 14x12
- SCREENED PORCH
- COVERED WALKWAY
- GARAGE 22x22

SECOND FLOOR:
- OPEN TO BELOW
- DECK BELOW
- LOFT 14x18
- OPEN TO BELOW
- ROOF BELOW

209—

FOCUSED ON THE OUT-
DOORS, THIS HOME WAS
BUILT AROUND VIEWS AND
OUTDOOR LIVING SPACES.

210

USED AS A MUSIC STUDIO, A SOFA BED ALLOWS THIS LOFTY AREA TO SERVE AS A GUEST ROOM.

Photography by F & E Schmidt

Photography by F & E Schmidt

THE KITCHEN, DINING ROOM, AND LIVING ROOM SHARE AN OPEN FLOOR PLAN, THOUGH ONE COULD HARDLY ARGUE THAT THEY'VE BEEN CROWDED TOGETHER. THE NATIVE AMERICAN DESIGN AND PRIMARY COLOR SCHEME TIE IN THROUGHOUT THE HOME. THE KITCHEN HAS LONG COUNTERTOPS ALLOWING THE CHEF TO SPREAD OUT. THE LIVING ROOM OPENS TO THE DECK OUTSIDE. IT HAS A VAULTED CEILING WITH LARGE WINDOWS THAT FILL THE HOME WITH FRESHNESS.

Photography by F & E Schmidt

THE KITCHEN DISPLAYS IT'S CHARM WITH THE USE OF OLD-FASHIONED APPLIANCES, PORCELAIN DOUBLE SINK, AND CERAMIC TILE ISLAND WITH HANGING POTS. A BRICK FLOOR ADDS COLOR AND TEXTURE TO THIS EARLY AMERICAN SETTING. AN EQUALLY CHARMING DINING ROOM HAS GORGEOUS STAINED GLASS FIXTURES.

Photography by F & E Schmidt

Photography by F & E Schmidt

THE DINING ROOM AND GREAT ROOM SHARE A RUSTIC, STONE MASONRY CHIMNEY AND ROARING FIRE. SPEC-
TACULAR CRAFTSMANSHIP WAS PUT TO TEST THROUGHOUT THE HOME, CREATING A HOME THAT IS BOTH
MAGNIFICENT IN DIMENSIONS AND MATERIALS, AND CHARMING IN THEIR USAGE.

Photography by F & E Schmidt

THE LOFT HAS BEEN FURNISHED AS A PRIVATE SITTING
AREA, DIVIDING AND UNITING SEPARATE GUEST SUITES.

THE CABIN'S MASTER BEDROOM AND BATH ARE ON THE FIRST FLOOR WITH SPECTACULAR MOUNTAINOUS VIEWS TO ENJOY WHILE RESTING AFTER A LONG DAY PLAYING ON THE FRONTIER.

219—

Familial Bliss

FIRST FLOOR

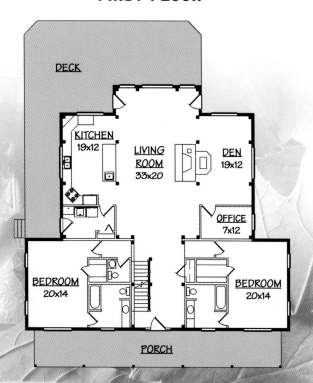

DECK

KITCHEN
19x12

LIVING
ROOM
33x20

DEN
19x12

OFFICE
7x12

BEDROOM
20x14

BEDROOM
20x14

PORCH

SECOND FLOOR

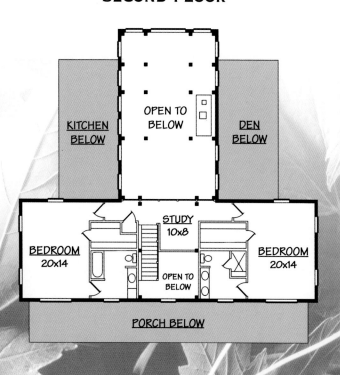

KITCHEN
BELOW

OPEN TO
BELOW

DEN
BELOW

BEDROOM
20x14

STUDY
10x8

OPEN TO
BELOW

BEDROOM
20x14

PORCH BELOW

What could be more conducive to family harmony than four separate retreats within one? Each member of the household has a private bedroom with bath, and the home is furnished with a study, an office, and a den where family members can retreat to read or work. If they need to cool their jets, there is a deck out back overlooking a waterfall, balm for any ailment. Most importantly, though, family members are lured together under a great cathedral ceiling, to a spacious living room and an open kitchen.

F & E Schmidt

A TWO-STORY TIMBER FRAME HOME WELCOMES GUESTS TO THE FRONT DOOR, WHERE THEY CAN SHELTER UNDER A FULL-LENGTH OVERHANG WHILE WAITING FOR THE DOORBELL'S EFFECT.

F & E Schmidt

A BACK DECK HUGS TWO SIDES OF THE HOUSE, AND IS MOST OFTEN UTILIZED AS AL FRESCO DINING ROOM, WEATHER PERMITTING. A PRIVATE WATERFALL IS A CONSTANT SOURCE OF SOOTHING INSPIRATION FOR FAMILY MEMBERS.

F & E Schmidt

AN INVITING FOYER WELCOMES GUESTS. A COLLECTION OF MIRRORS AFFORDS FAMILY
MEMBERS A FINAL HAIR CHECK BEFORE THEY LEAVE.

225

F & E Schmidt

THE STUDY AREA UPSTAIRS WAS FURNISHED WITH STURDY ANTIQUES THAT
HAVE WITHSTOOD THE TEST OF PREVIOUS FAMILIES.

THERE ARE FOUR BEDROOMS THROUGHOUT THE HOME, THIS ONE FURNISHED FOR
THE YOUNGEST FAMILY MEMBER, COMPLETE WITH A WHIMSICAL MURAL.

227—

AN AWE-INSPIRING LIVING ROOM, KITCHEN AREA IS DOMINATED
BY A STONE HEARTH. AN INCREDIBLE VIEW IS FILTERED IN
THROUGH TRIPLE-TIERED WINDOWS AND INTRICATE WOOD BEAM
STRUCTURE.

F & E Schmidt

THE KITCHEN AND DINING ROOM BOTH HAVE LIGHT WOOD CABINETRY AND FURNISHINGS IN KEEPING WITH THE REST OF THE HOUSE. BY STACKING THREE WALLS WITH CABINETRY AND APPLIANCES, THE HOMEOWNERS WERE ABLE TO DEFINE THE KITCHEN'S FOURTH WALL WITH AN ISLAND, SO THE COOK NEVER FEELS ISOLATED FROM THE FAMILY BEYOND.

Born in a Barn

Two homes, one great retreat, this family enjoys both a log home with their primary living quarters, and a beautiful timber frame barn where they can get away for an intense workout or a truly quiet and comfortable escape. The owner, a builder, also has an office in the barn. For a passerby, the property appears to be a historic landmark or a well-preserved working farm. The hidden intent, however, is pure modern comfort.

A HUMBLE LOOKING TWO-STORY LOG HOME AND A TRADITIONAL-RED BARN ARE WHAT PASSERBY SEE OF THIS WONDERFUL HOME. ON THE FAR SIDE OF THE BARN, THOUGH, IS A PURELY MODERN BANK OF WINDOWS THAT ILLUMINATES AN INTERIOR NOT DEDICATED TO AGRICULTURE. A SMALL PORTION OF THE BARN WAS DEVOTED TO HOUSING FOR PRIZE-WINNING HORSES.

Rich Frutchey

EXPOSED LOG ADDS WARMTH AND SOLIDITY TO THE
FAMILY ROOM IN THE MAIN HOUSEHOLD.

Rich Frutchey

BLUE CABINETRY ADDS COLOR AND CHARMING COUNTRY ACCENT TO A WOOD-RICH KITCHEN AND DINING ROOM.

—236

237—

Upstairs bedrooms honor an equestrian passion.

Rich Frutchey

A LOFTY BEDROOM ALLOWS DREAMS TO SOAR. A BANK OF WINDOWS SHEDS LIGHT ON A LIVING AREA WHERE A WEAVER PLIES HER CRAFT, AND AN ENORMOUS RECREATION AREA AND GYM.

Rich Frutchey